A CAT FOR ALL SEASONS

JOAN CAMPBELL

First Published in 2016 by
For The Right Reasons
60 Grant St, Inverness, IV3 8BS
Tel: 01463 718844 or 07717457247
Email: fortherightreasons@rocketmail.com

ISBN: 978-1-910205-88-4

British Library Cataloguing-in-Publication Data
A catalogue record of this book is available from
The British Library

CONTENTS

Lona Johnson
Regional Development Officer
Highlands & Islands
Cats Protection.

I first became aware of Joan Campbell when she applied to become a volunteer for the Caithness Branch of Cats Protection in the spring of 2012. She and her friend Vicky Hill were specifically interested in helping local feral cats (wild living cats of domestic ancestry) by undertaking a programme of trap, neuter and return (TNR). Once adult these cats are as wild as the iconic Scottish Wildcat, and will not adapt to a domestic environment, so attempting to tame them would be contrary to their welfare. Returning them to site also prevents other cats from moving into the area (which would be the case if the cats were removed altogether) and TNR leads to a stable and relatively healthy cat population. In contrast to this approach, one unneutered female cat can, in five years, be responsible for 20,000 descendants, leading to associated problems relating to cat welfare and nuisance to nearby human populations.

As can be imagined although extremely rewarding, TNR can be a difficult and demanding role, requiring the volunteers to be out in all weathers, lifting heavy equipment and dealing with anxious or aggressively frightened cats. Old clothes, wellies and waterproofs are therefore de rigeur for these brave individuals. Although not expecting Joan to turn up to a branch meeting dressed for the hills, I was nonetheless somewhat disconcerted to meet this tall, slim and immaculately dressed lady at the AGM and, I freely admit, wondered if she knew what she was letting herself in for. At the time I had not read Joan's two excellent previous books, "Heads on Pillows" and "Bye Bye B&B" so was unaware that she is of crofting stock and has wrestled recalcitrant lambing ewes (whilst cooking an evening meal for her B&B guests without them becoming aware of the on-going midwifery), coped with an "idiosyncratic" horse and been the proud owner of one of the first ever house rabbits. A few stroppy felines were therefore never going to pose much problem for Joan.

5

The fact that she is a "local lassie" and knows the local landscape like the back of her hand, not to mention probably every human being in a 5 mile radius, has proven to be a distinct advantage in finding and helping the local feral cat populations. Additionally Joan's background in running a B&B, one of the most demanding service industries, plus her time promoting tourism and sitting on a variety of committees, has given her paramount people skills, very useful when not only persuading the landowners to have the cats on their land neutered, but also to have them back afterwards.

Between them I think that Joan and Vicky have now taken just about every feral in the Melvich area to the vets for neutering and rumour has it that the local menfolk are starting to look nervous, as Joan has been heard to remark that "if it moves, we'll neuter it".

Whether you are new to Joan's books, or have read the previous two in the series, I hope that you will enjoy "a Cat for all Seasons". The book covers a wide period with anecdotes from throughout Joan's adult life, but was written after Joan and "Himself" sold the B&B. It is funny, irreverent and occasionally very touching. Long may she continue to write about her life and, of course, to help cats in the Melvich area and beyond. Enjoy!

A Cat For All Seasons

*'The greatness of a nation and its moral progress can be judged
by the way its animals are treated.'*
Mahatma Gandhi

Introduction

So, the B&B is sold, against big odds. The new house is built, against bigger odds, much to the chagrin of the cats who all thought the emerging home was merely a large and interesting adventure play-ground that kept them amused for months. Then they saw the furniture move in. Disbelief and anarchy took over. Why leave a perfectly comfortable billet and a wonderful wild-life garden for a suspiciously weird new build...in a quarry? Smudge blamed me, taking sweet revenge on the whole project, Pooh blaming The Hobbit, never uttering a civil meow to him since. The Hobbit? Well, he being a stoical creature, he got on with it, as did I, there being no other option. And getting on with it should have been that longed for haven of retreat well away from days woven round the needs of others rather than my own desires, and no doubt totally selfish ambitions, shelved in anticipation of that retirement. And at last I was almost there.

So what did I do? I lost the plot completely and back I went to pick up the gauntlet I had laid at the foot of one of the most difficult boards I ever served upon. Not that my colleagues were the problem. It was the sums. I had never been good at sums and the sums this board debated were of a different magnitude altogether. And of course, I spent more time with my mouth open, saying 'What?' than learning my sums. When I left, with inappropriate glee according to a friend still soldering on, after doing the stint I had been inveigled into believing this would be a great service to the tourism industry, I celebrated long and hard, determined to blank out my persuasive arguments that saw the board spend unbelievable millions on what was for me an exciting tourism project, drawing fears, tears and cheers in equal measure. My hangover was a punishing three year contract in their employ. How did that happen? Me! Working for some of the academics I had despaired of ever being able to understand?

Putting our Guest House on the market had given me the honourable excuse to ditch the tentacles of tourism that had slowly begun to strangle me. It got me out of a handful of boards and committees and allowed me to dream about freedom. It was a dream soon to be shattered, what with the housing market collapsing, the cost of new build going through the roof, and investments crashing to a new low at every squirm of the Footsie. The chaos that was 2008 caught up with my well planned future and led me to believe that redemption lay in this offer of employment I was intrigued by, dangled in front of my nose with the promise of not a lot of work attached to quite a lot of money. How the reverse came about I'm not quite sure. No doubt my tendency to nod the head when I should be shaking it influenced the outcome.

No option then, if I were to be worthy of my meagre pay slip but to throw my time into the project with gay abandonment. This meant a long crawl back into nooks and crannies of tourism I had cocked a snoop at, a necessary exercise if I wanted to keep up with the ever-changing platform I was to dance upon as the person providing the link between the industry and academia in the build of a BA Degree in Tourism & Hospitality Practice for the University of the Highlands & Islands. At the time of my tentative start, the

University had yet to gain full title and my ability to assist with the degree became a small cog in the essentials governing that necessity. So no pressure then.

Limping to the end of that contract, emotionally battered and somewhat worn out, yet inordinately chuffed at achieving validation for the degree against odds even bigger than life was chucking at me in our attempt to juggle finance round new build, and fund the cost of selling, I was more than ready for that elusive retirement. You would think by now I had learned enough to keep my mouth shut and appreciate the peace and quiet needed to fulfil this life-long dream of spending my days as a writer rather than bedding my regular column into a terror-crazed deadline, and moaning to any who cared to ask about the next book, 'I wish I had the time. I just never seem to get time to do anything, I'm so busy doing everything!' I knew exactly what I meant but didn't have time to edify and generally met a response of, 'But I thought you were retired.'

'I am. And I will be when I get time,' my reply imbued with a genuine frown brought about more by puzzlement than annoyance. Nor did it help to know that time was not as plentiful as it had been, not according to the good book's idea of allocation of years.

So, did I keep my mouth shut? No, not at all! At my very last, and this time determined that last meant final, committee meeting with VisitScotland, in front of a whole host of people with sensible retirement plans, I was asked the inevitable question, 'What on earth will you find to do with your time now?'

'Oh, I'm going to work with cats. Cats will be much easier to herd than people!' I heard myself announce to all and sundry. For one mad moment I looked as stunned as my audience, thinking, did I say that or was it the woman beside me. But the seed was sown.

So here I am, exchanging cats for people, adamant that I'm doing no paper-work and must have as little to do with people as is humanly possible. My sole ambition is to be a hands-on volunteer worker with feral cats, get them to the vet on time, and go home, job done. No more worries. Sleep peacefully every night. Concentrate on my next book. You would think, living with Smudge for so many years, I would have been put off cats for life, but no. Obviously, I had more lessons to learn. Problem is, I just need to see a cat and I'm half in love with it. I don't feel that way about people and they don't feel that way about me. Nor do cats.

In a small community it doesn't take long to find out whether you're actually doing a job well done, or causing the inevitable head-shaking scepticism I somehow seem to attract. I journey through life under the strong impression that other people do jobs well done. I raise eyebrows. Take yesterday for instance.

'The children are not very happy.'

'Why?' I asked, bending over to pick up the trap with its latest incumbent hissing its objection as I listened to the voice of those who believe you should be privy to what's being bandied about, especially if it's about you.

'The children are fond of the cats.'

'Aw, that's nice. They are so good to the ferals, feeding them,' I enthused. They are lovely children. I'd read passages from my cat book, The Land Beyond The Green Fields, to the older children in the local primary school, and wrote a cat story with pictures so the infants would not be left out. Their enthusiasm for cats and their own stories about their pets took over and the rest of my time at the school was spent without having to read another word. It's amazing how children, like

10

animals, can manipulate me out of what I intend doing and into exactly what they want me to do. And that day it was: listen to their stories. That, no doubt, was why I got the biggest cheer, with whispered assurances of, 'You're our favourite author!' OK, it was some time since they had an author read to them, but they meant well and I had no wish to get on their wrong side in this new job that brought me under close scrutiny.

'Aye, but you take the cats away, and the children don't like it,' the gruff voice continued to castigate.

'But I bring them back.' It was part of the deal.

'The children say you're killing the cats.'

'What?' I gasped, mouth wide open in disbelief.

I had fully explained the routine. The cats all had to come back to be released where they were picked up. It was part of the Cats Protection TNR programme. Trap, neuter and return. I had emphasised how this would ensure good health in the colony and everyone who said they were worried about the feral cats and their growing number of kittens had been adamant they wanted no more kittens running amuck. I wanted cats who could sidle up and whisper in a feline ear, 'You have nothing to worry about, my pretty. I've had the operation!' I was assured the black cat with the white collar, locally known as The Minister, and his two side-kicks, a big, black tom and a wild looking striped grey tomcat went about with permanent grins on their faces while the females spent their time heavily pregnant or nursing bedraggled kittens, possibly replicating life as it was for many a female about a century ago in the very same village.

I slunk off, muttering to myself as I closed the car boot on my catch for the day, 'Cruella De Vil of the cat world. Bloody great!' Just what I needed as my first interaction with a community abandoned for the last twenty years to devote *myself to tourism. Upsetting the local children. A cat killer. The road ahead suddenly seemed less rosy than I had painted it when I donned the Cats Protection sweatshirt with a sense of pride. Like so many bright notions that mark the road I travel upon, it seemed a very good idea at the time.*

Chapter 1

Behold the iguana puffing itself out to make itself a man.

South African Proverb

Night Of The Iguana

'There's a smell of cat's pee on this loaf.' He sniffed hard, suspicious that the shopping had shared the car with a boot full of feral cats. It had, but isolated in the back seat, well away from any prospect of spraying through the dust sheets commandeered to cover the traps.

'There most certainly is not,' I countered, indignant at the very thought. 'It's many long years since you smelled cat's pee in our house!' Himself, this man of my dreams, occasional nightmares, and eventual supporter of most of my bright ideas, was wary. It had to do with cats. Not that he dislikes cats, but in the distant past, when we were endeavouring to get to know each other, he insisted he was a dog man. Yet, when I defied his best advice and brought a dog into our lives, that venture did not measure up to his expectations of how a new bride should behave. However, that was a long time ago, long before Smudge entered our lives and taught us the deviousness of a bright-eyed, albeit squint-eyed, cat. And long before I had backup – that one fine son we produced over a period of fun-filled years trying for this elusive family. It turned out our son was as determined as I that animals are good for the stability and wellbeing of a household. I imbued this small child with such logic at an early age and, bless him, he used it against me at every opportunity since; the things that were good for his wellbeing became legion, until he produced a family of his own. Then his wellbeing took on a change of attitude.

To be titled Himself, or if deeds allow, Herself, in any good Highland homestead, must by necessity be won through many years of proving to your peers you are head of the household. My husband had, somehow, through time, achieved this distinction. In order to give him the anonymity he demanded when he first suspected I had the temerity to write about real live happenings in our busy bed and breakfast home, he insisted, 'You're not putting my name into that...' a short soul-searching interlude before continuing '...stuff you're writing.' It was before I had a publisher so he felt reasonably confident, but just to be on the safe side, the warning was issued.

I replied with disarming honesty, 'Your name will not sully these pages.' He smirked, forgetting I had years of experience of counter-balancing his natural reservations with my exuberance that allowed him his reserve and me my interaction with people. He never again mentioned the matter in the sure conviction this venture was most unlikely to see the light of day. But it did, and how could the story be told without Himself. Anyway, had he been kept out of the picture, I have a feeling he would have been quite miffed.

He had agreed with my passionate argument that we should have animals about the place and proceeded to fill our lives with sheep. That was not what I meant. Our growing son had no more liking than I had to work with sheep so we countered with horses, to enrich the lives of the cats, dogs and rabbits furtively added to the stock while Himself slaved away on distant shores, unsuspecting. He was so glad to be home every now and again, he accepted these sudden additions to the family. I was convinced all animals thrown together should get along, just as I believed all nature of people should cooperate likewise when hanging out under the one roof.

A foolish notion on both counts.

But hey, life goes on and you make the best of whatever situation you create, or so I kept telling myself as I dealt with the various results.

This latest venture of mine involving cats, when I broached the subject, was initially met with suspicion, then, surprise, surprise, if not exactly encouragement, it wasn't the usual hands thrown out wide gesture followed by a lecture on all that could, and most decidedly would, go wrong! Why? Because this time I have a secret weapon.

My secret weapon is not a member of our family, that tribe across the road as Himself is wont to dub them. Not Katrina, our son's affianced partner and mother of our grandchildren, a staunch ally, and up for it, most of the time. Life without her would be a sad thing. Himself views their escapades with the same scepticism as he views my ventures into the unknown. People who do not have his direct bloodline, allowing right of passage to his favours are liked, or disliked, according to a warm and friendly attitude to most people, an extraordinary liking for some, coupled with an adamant refusal to bother with any who stand on his toes. What puzzles me is, this toe standing must be done by remote control as, since retiring from his arduous work in the oil fields, he views social interaction as occasions to avoid, unless carried out under his own roof. Then it's open arms and everyone's welcome, or accusing glances cast in my direction, 'Why didn't they come? What did you do to them?'

He is a deeply loyal man. When he approves of and likes someone, in his eyes they do little wrong. That is the case with our young neighbours, Vicky and James, friends of Neil and Katrina, and our grandchildren Shane, at the time of writing, 14 years old, and Fallon, a very responsible eight. Not that Shane is irresponsible, quite the contrary, but he does have a wild streak in him, its source an arguable point when concern is voiced: 'Are you forgetting what you were like yourself,' pitched into the debate by a grandfather who cannot see him do

15

wrong once he came to terms with the unbelievable naughtiness a small child can wreak, he being away from home during many of his own son's growing years.

I remember Neil at a young age taking to the hills from where he at intervals shouted down to his father, 'Is it safe to come home yet?' after breaking a large pane of the garage window within close proximity to his father's wrath. Then, when Shane, who despite being only two was extremely active and work orientated, took a trowel from the shed and with tremendous gusto weeded out his grandfather's newly emerging regimented rows of carrots, the air turned the same delicate shade of blue as when my baby house rabbit was encouraged to go out and enjoy the pleasures of the garden. Rex took to pruning the young carrots with a greed beyond his size and nibbled through their disciplined ranks with such ferocity, the denuded stumps proved impossible to camouflage. There was no hiding place for me or the rabbit, but Himself got over these disruptions, and now as Shane grows and ventures forth, testing the perimeters of his parent's guidance, his faux pas are met with his grandfather's indulgent smile.

As a two year old who viewed Toad of Toad Hall as his out-and-out hero, Shane was overjoyed to discover Toad's car sitting outside his Nana's place of work. Excitement grew when the owner of the ancient vehicle, a man of some eminence in the community, appeared in a tweed cape and hat with tie-down ear flaps, just like Toad wore when wreaking havoc upon the countryside. 'Mr Toad,' the excited child shouted. 'Mr Toad!'

The man, who was in his normal attire had been treating the residents of a Thurso care home to a short ride in his beautiful vintage vehicle, took no offence. 'I suppose I do look a little like him,' he responded and gave Shane a ride he never forgot. Shane's inclination to see cartoon characters emerge from the personalities around him, accompanied by a reasonable ability to mimic, could have arisen from that act of kindness. About the same time, he greatly admired the irascibility of Samuel Whiskers and his wife Anna-Maria whose tail always stuck out from behind her long dresses. When I was assuring his mother I was spending quality time with him, I could sneak in a half hour's work by sticking Samuel Whiskers or Toad of Toad Hall on the telly, nipping back and fore to assure him, 'Yes, of course they're real. Toad lives in Wick and Samuel's got a hole under the floor boards. But they don't come out in case Smudge gets them.' That he could relate to. Smudge had him completely under her rule and never forgave Katrina for usurping her kittens' position by producing a kitten of her own.

Then one day I had a colleague visit, and Shane seemed fascinated with Anne-Marie, keeping circling her as I showed her to her car. 'Where does her keep hers tail?' he wanted to know as we walked back to the house. I realised it was time I stopped encouraging his vivid imagination, especially after he pled with his father to bore a hole in their skirting boards so that his Granny and Papa could live there when they were old!

Happily, our grandchildren love Vicky and James, who breathed fresh air into the empty property, Fairview, located between our two family homes: Stoneybraes, our house built for that glorious retirement after selling The Sheiling B&B, where I am supposed to repose in splendid tranquillity, and the house Neil built for his family. At the end of the undertaking Neil appeared to be too traumatised to find a name for the house. So that he didn't have to stress himself when internet shopping demands a name for your property, they seem happy enough styling their address after the number belonging to the croft land the house sits upon, so No.57 it became. It still is, 12 years down the line.

Fairview was the original Campbell homestead and remained so until Jock, Himself's uncle, died, well into old age. The first six years of our married life were spent sharing

17

the same roof as this elderly bachelor, his affable collie Glen, and a front porch full of sacks of sheep food, much to my horror, having had no notion of crofting life and such idiosyncrasies until I was taken to stay there as a very young bride. We built our own first home, The Sheiling, on the croft just up the hill from Fairview and moved in there the year Neil was born. To ensure we benefited from the outstanding view, we built on an old site filled with massive boulders, all that was left of what was said to be the first village school, in effect, a thatched low-roofed stone building where the family lived. Removing the massive stones was almost as arduous as tackling the self-build. One stone had the inscription 1866 carved into its granite surface.

I was assured the old house had been a home used to the laughter of children, referred to as Marag and Katag's, two sisters who initiated teaching to the young of the community. And if you believe such things, happiness continued to permeate from the foundations into the newly built walls whenever children came about The Sheiling. Despite my inability to produce more than the one specimen, my siblings all added their offspring to the mix, Magnus, after marrying my friend Donella, managing to become the father of triplet daughters at the tender age of eighteen years!

I worked as a secretary at the nearby atomic energy establishment at Dounreay when an unexpected call came from my older sister, Sandra. 'Donella's had a girl. The baby came early so she was rushed to Raigmore because they think it's twins.'

What a surprise. That was the kind of medical care we got in the sticks then. With a promise to phone me back, I waited with baited breath.

'It's another girl,' Sandra's voice shaking with excitement. 'There might be another one,' and she was gone, my cries of 'What?' ignored while colleagues clustered round.

I couldn't have heard right they said. But I did. I waited and waited. Nothing more.

I was beside myself with anxiety and putting a call out was not to be encouraged. Eventually I made the call and a stunned voice told me, 'Oh, yes, she's had another little girl!' Sandra was so shocked she forgot to phone back. Magnus was at sea on our father's seine netter, fishing somewhere in the Pentland Firth, when the radio crackled into life and stunned the entire crew! To go from expecting a child in six week's time to the father of three in one radio communication took a bit of convincing. Donella, bless her and her triple bundles, took it all in her capable stride, as she does all that comes her way. That week, Sandra and I travelled with Magnus, along with his sister-in-law and husband to see Donella and her surprise delivery, this being long before IVF intervention, bringing the media in as identical triplets were so unusual in that day. But cars, not babies, took over the en route conversation. Then, turning round to look at us, and referring to Sandra, Magnus said, 'That one is built for comfort,' then pointing at me, 'And that one's built for speed.' Sort of summed us up.

When my only child asked the inevitable question, 'Why am I the only one with no brothers or sisters?' I parried with, 'Because I went for quality rather than quantity,' allowing him to view me from an early age with more than a little of his father's scepticism. 'Are you sure you know what you're doing,' was a familiar response to the road ahead, as I saw it.

Jock remained at Fairview, taking a wily delight in shocking the neighbourhood by marrying his lady friend at the ripe old age of 80! I was delighted for them, liking them both. By then Jock had handed over the croft land to Himself who in time built up a flock of sheep, keeping the old man happy as sheep had been his life's work after retiring at an early age from the Police Force to help care for aging parents. When

Jock died, the house, naturally, went into the family of his widow and on her death, it lay empty for many years then selling on to two different owners before Vicky and James arrived. They are a quiet young couple so we never got to know them during their first year there, not until we moved into our new home situated just above The Sheiling, built with our needs in mind, rather than that of a houseful of paying guests.

'If you had four legs and a tail, Joan would have got to know you far sooner,' Himself assured them.

Running a busy guest house, as I'd done for all of 40 years, began to seriously restrict our social life, quite unlike the early years when family and guests got together for ceilidhs. Like the night the iguana arrived, a full-blown party reverberating into the wee small hours, was probably the main reason I was quite unaware of its presence in the house. It had no reservation and every intention of settling in for at least 10 days! It was an interesting enough creature, green, with a very long tongue, like an envious friend who often had too much to say about mutual friends. She was not one of my favourites. Nor was the iguana.

When the family left, after waving a cheery goodbye, I hastened to do their room. There was the iguana, grinning at me, from its perch on the sunny windowsill. Panic stations set in! How far down the line would they be before remembering it? Would I have been the cause of its demise by then as I had no idea how to even lift the creature, leave alone toilet and feed the thing. They lived in England and an early start gave them one overnight close to the Borders. Their iguana was on the north coast seaboard, probably wondering why?

Was it dumped!

Before I succumbed to a nervous wreck, the boy came back, casually sauntering down the corridor to pick up his wee pal. He had left it to get the best of the early morning sun while they said goodbye to the Kingtons who lived up the road

20

and were the reason they holidayed in Melvich. This was in the very early days, even before I gave hospitality to my first guest dog, and despite always hoping a cat may arrive unexpectedly, one never ever did. When I took my first tentative steps towards plying people with hospitality so I could take money off them, all I had was a baby and a dog, and a bit of a cheek.

We made the most of Christmases and winter opportunities for socialising, but other times were difficult so we were determined that Stoneybraes would allow the hospitality we offered strangers for so many years. This time, friends and family are the undisputed recipients. And that is how we got to know Vicky and James, introduced by Neil and Katrina all of three years ago. Vicky is my secret weapon.

Chapter 2

'Cats know how to obtain food without labour, shelter without confinement, and love without penalties.'

W. L. George

Herding Cats

A short time ago, after the sun had made sufficient progress over the yardarm to allow me believe it was time to charge a couple of glasses with wine, Himself asked for the umpteenth time, 'Does that mean you're out of everything to do with tourism?'

I sighed. We had this conversation often. Desperate to move on from many of my commitments, each time I came home cock-a-hoop to announce, 'Well, that's the last time I'll have to do that,' Himself would look suitably impressed and ask, 'Is that it then?' But it never was. I had given up most of my volunteer tourism work but wanted to stay with the Federation of Small Businesses, doing their regional secretarial work, and this would take a bit of talking up, over a glass of quality wine, on one of the few balmy autumn evenings of 2012. Of course, when it came to a real hard sell on a winter's night, a cosy peat fire with a glass of port helped put across my view. Himself can be hard to convince at times. Probably because my intention to leave the Highlands & Islands Tourism Awards board I sit on since its inauguration lacked conviction and to be encouraged from these demanding posts, you usually have to seriously piss off your colleagues, which I have managed to avoid...to date.

It's work I don't want to walk away from, strengthened as it is by today's ease of communication through multi-media facilities, and the pleasure of working with people who have become more than colleagues makes all the difference in the world. And Himself knows well, this passion to approve quality tourism runs through my veins.

But so too does a life-long love of cats. I know, Smudge, like a wayward child, commands exasperated attention, but that does not debar love. She somehow had our devotion for her entire life. Along with her incredible demands, she set her sights on wooing the man Himself, and that achievement in itself gave her unbelievable kudos. And she did this without ever uttering a meow. Smudge achieved much without mewing or purring, yet her face could beam with satisfaction, or dance with devilment. Those were her two expressions. And she could spit for Scotland! I swear she would sit in a corner practicing when nothing we could see was bothering her.

I explained, 'No, that is not it. It's just one more responsibility I can set aside. Honestly, I won't be doing that again, but I will be working with the FSB, and the tourism awards board, you know that.'

He screwed up blue eyes that still sparkle despite his advancing years, obviously concerned. 'So despite all you said, you'll still be involved in tourism.'

'Only a bit.' I smiled across at him. 'This is a lovely wine, would you like a top up? Oh, good. Actually I won't have that much time for tourism work. There's my next book, and the garden to sort out, and this is a big house to look after, and, well, you see, I'm going to be working with cats.'

There, I said it.

'Cats?' Anxiety immediately clouded his face. 'What cats? Haven't we enough cats here.' Poodie-Pooh, Smudge's daughter, was hugging the arm of his chair. He insisted she did not spread her ample backside upon his knee and said I was too soft with her each time I despaired of removing her white hairs from my black suits. Her brother, The Hobbit was fully stretched out at his feet, long striped legs twitching as he dreamed about his days as a top class rabbiter. By now, Smudge had wreaked her revenge on our move to Stoneybraes and was gone from our hearth, if not our hearts.

'Not our cats. Feral cats. Vicky and I are going to join Cats Protection and trap cats.' It sounded evil, but it was what she and I agreed upon, each of us desperate not to touch paperwork, having enough in our everyday lives to steer our good intentions into the one and only skill we felt acceptable to Janis and the CP Caithness committee who viewed their new recruits with a hint of unease. Vicky dressed from her office job, me coming straight from a meeting. So OK, we didn't exactly look the part, but we had the bit between our teeth, and that is what we wanted to be. Trappers!

Himself's frown disappeared. 'Vicky's doing this with you?' I didn't need to say much more before snagging a genuine interest when I explained about the huge colony of feral cats in Portskerra that required serious attention. He's a great believer in supporting a local cause, so long as it's me doing the hands-on work and him doing the home-based encouragement. Take going to church. He seems to think I can pave his way to Heaven, provided he encourages, and I keep up the attendances.

The crofting villages of Portskerra and Melvich are separated by Melvich Hotel. Melvich runs along the border of the main road west from the town of Thurso, this long drawn out village ending at the junction of the Hotel, whereas Portskerra is located around its own ring-road branching off the A836. A teasing rivalry between the villages is diluted to non-existence today. When I first came to live here, each vied with the other to claim the name of the most hospitable, and the many who offered one room for bed and breakfast in their homes during the peak summer months were known for their kindness and welcoming attitude.

For me Portskerra was the winner because two of my friends lived there, Lal and Clare. And so many homes, including theirs, had old matriarchs who made you tremendously welcome and had great stories of how things used to be, and of course, were thoroughly versed in the local gossip delivered with the power to enthral. Entertainment found at one's own fireside was rated far higher than any TV soap opera, few of us owning a TV when I first stayed in the village with Clare, or Lal, teenagers with fun in mind, then as young newlyweds still with fun in mind, but no money in our pockets for such luxuries as TVs. I soon got to know Barbara and Joey finding outstanding warmth and hospitality at their hearth, and they lived in Melvich. Mind you, they originally came from Portskerra! However, the Campbell family whose hospitality and welcome into their fold could not be faulted, were rooted in Melvich for generations back on the paternal side. I was blessed from the first day I set foot over their threshold with the finest mother-in-law who ever lived. Rhoda Campbell, gone now, had delighted her huge family by living into her very late nineties, after arriving in Melvich as a young relative of the Hotel Manageress and finding a husband as well as work at the village's highly respected hostelry hosting the landed gentry in their sporting pursuits, and paying good heed to the needs of the locality. My own mother actually met Rhoda there during a short spell of work before she decamped as a young girl to Edinburgh to find work and a husband although he actually came from Kirtomy, a few miles west of Melvich, and east of her own small coastal village of Scullomie. A happy meeting in a world not quite so small in those days.

She told me Rhoda was a tiny woman, and extremely pretty, known by the staff as 'Toddling Bonny'! The man she married came from a big family, in stature as well as number but he was the only one of several sons to delight his parents with grandchildren. Sadly, he was the only one too, who succumbed to cancer at a young age and died before I met his son, leaving Rhoda with a grown family of two sons and four daughters ready to make their way in the world.

As in most communities along our seaboard, everyone knew everyone else then and there was never a need to lock, or knock at, doors. The local police station, shoulder to shoulder with the District Nurse's house, were located in Melvich, giving the village a bit of status. The Portskerra folks just said there was much need of them there! Now the Police Station is privately owned and the Nurse's house a store for National Health stock. How times have changed.

When we first decided to build our own home, I suggested we relocate to Portskerra, isolated as I was by having only elderly neighbours. The fun always happened in Portskerra. Parochialism hit a high as Himself became panic struck at the prospect and went to great lengths to ensure we sourced land in Melvich. Jock came to his rescue and assigned the tenancy of the croft to him resolving the problem and fulfilling a prophesy made by an old, and rather strange person who once worked as the handyman at Melvich Hotel.

He had the reputation of second sight and spent a lot of time sighing to himself with tears in his eyes. One day he looked through me and into a distance I knew nothing of.

'You're going to move from that house,' he suddenly announced, pinning me to the spot. We were living in Fairview and very happy with it.

'Definitely not!' I asserted. He got that one wrong for sure.

'You won't go far. Then you'll go again. You won't go far again. But you'll go up. Up.' And then he moved on, coal scuttle in hand, oblivious to my consternation. No way were we moving from Jock's after all the work Himself put in to allow us our separate quarters which were working out well. I loved the place and by then persuaded Jock that the front porch was not quite the place to stack dusty hessian sacks of

26

sheep feed. I worried then in case this strange man was merely pointing out my inability to go far in life. But eventually, I would be going up! Neither tourism nor ambition had entered into my soul then so neither going far nor going up meant much to my daily musings.

'Listen,' I said when I got home. 'Old Jock at the Hotel says we'll be moving from here.'

I liked to give my new husband something to think about. He, with a mouthful of nails and a hammer in his hand, paused, looked at me hard, laid down the hammer and removed the nails. 'No. I don't think we'll be doing that any time soon. Although I always fancied New Zealand myself. What about a cup of tea?' And that was an end to that. Until six years later we moved up the hill, and 42 years after that, we moved further up the hill, cats and all, but have yet to set foot in New Zealand.

Chapter 3

'One cat just leads to another.'

Ernest Hemmingway

The Territorial Cat

Growing up in the small village of Kirtomy, not that far from Melvich, in a family of three girls and two boys, with a mother who stayed at home because that was the done thing, and a father who was seldom at home because the sea had been his life before the second world war, during the war, and after the war earning his keep with the fishing boats that kept him from hearth and home for six days out of every seven during our early upbringing.

We were, akin to most families we knew, loved and cared for without question, nor was there any need to be constantly told so. About being wanted, well, there were times when we certainly were not, chucked out from under the feet into all kinds of weather and thinking nothing of it. Nor were we demonstratively hugged and pampered any more than were our playmates. But we were secure and can look back on a happy childhood with boundaries well marked and sufficient nous not to let an adult know when we strayed over borderlines. A hand was not spared and could be administered by any mother who saw fit without the threat of reprisal from an indignant parent. I do not recall the weight of a masculine hand, not even our father's in anger, excepting the Headmaster, but he was a teacher, and they were viewed as ruling from a higher sphere, their actions beyond question.

We did our fair share of asserting our rights with siblings and playmates alike but blood was always thicker than water and carrying tales was a heinous crime. The first person to clip us on the ear and send us on our way was usually the person we appraised of whatever deed considered so dastardly it was worth the risk of the retribution that weighed upon our squealer heads. Loving the wild open spaces, I spent as much time out of doors as I could squeeze out of the day, my constant playmate a boy of my own age and tastes in how that day should be used.

Every homestead had cats, but the majority of dogs we knew belonged to those who had working crofts and they were collies, most to be avoided, like Ben from across the burn, parading his territory on the Overside, putting us in fear of a nip on the heels, or worse, if we ventured too noisily towards his domain.

Ben once had the temerity to make his way from his home, strutting down the road towards the burn that divides Kirtomy in two. Our home was on the west side set among a string of homesteads, spread well enough apart to afford privacy, yet sufficiently close to shout a greeting, or wave a fist, land then being of no premium to people who had the tenancy of adjoining parcels of ground known as crofts. This was long before people came from the south and viewed this largesse with envious disbelief, setting them off on the long road to coveting what was not ours to give but belonged to the Landlords of the day, who cared little what was done with it, so long as it was not a claim to ownership.

Beneath the single track road more fields gently roll down towards the burn graduating to very steep braes the further up the burn you come. Ben stayed about half a mile away as the crow flies. When we took it into our heads to visit Ben's home, we too could go as the crow flies, if we were prepared to take the risk of using the shortcut down Merran's Brae, much to her chagrin, our trespassing ending in strident shouts of, 'Get off my land!' The wings of the crow lent speed to our heels, in case our mothers heard Merran's screams of righteous anger and then we would have to answer for setting the old woman off, much depending upon the temper she happened to be in that particular day. That our mothers made much use of this shortcut, as often as not to similar howls of belligerence, was considered none of our business.

My father's cat, the black and white cat, brooked nonsense from none, especially a dog. She watched Ben's approach from the top of the dyke that separated our garden from the road. Without more ado, off she set down Merran's Brae gathering speed the closer Ben got to the burn, reaching it just as Ben had the audacity to set paw upon the bridge. And there was Merran, arms akimbo, standing watching the black and white cat making good use of her land. We stood transfixed with terror for our cat and fear of Merran's reaction if we headed after the cat. Then in the middle of the bridge there was a great stand-off while our hearts thumped in fear as our cat, back arched and tail bristling, stood up to this very large and very hostile dog. I don't remember who struck the first blow but to our great relief the ensuing melee ended in Ben howling his way back home accompanied by our cheers for the battle was loud and long and at times I despaired for the cat.

Apparently there was an audience on the Overside too and we were talked to about the behaviour of our cat but we saw her as the heroine, tail held high, proudly marching back up the shortcut having dealt with the would-be intruder. Merran nodded her head to us and repaired to her fireside, a satisfied look upon her face. She had no wish to see a dog from the Overside take liberties that could involve her own dog, Swannie. It says a lot for our upbringing that we never heard our parents, despite at times being frustrated beyond measure, refer to both female occupants of that little half house as bitches!

Early one summer morning, a huge swan invaded our garden causing no end of excitement until the black and white cat arrived, tail high and hair rising stiffly. After an alarming skirmish she saw off the swan. I still have a mental picture of its massive wingspan as it raced down the garden for take-off with our bold cat in hot pursuit. Sadly, some days later the swan was found dead in the upper waters of the burn.

'Did you not know, cat, swans are protected birds,' she was told but she didn't care. Nor did she mind not having a proper name, just the black and white cat. I often wondered in years to come, if she came back to haunt me in the form of the only other black and white cat I ever fell for, the incorrigible Smudge, named before I had the wit to stop myself, and we all know, once you name an animal, you end up with it! But who needed a dog when our bold black and white cat was there to protect her family! Some time after that, she succumbed to feline influenza, or maybe it was bird flu, before we knew it existed. My mother, whom I always felt could be strict with the cats, nursed her assiduously with warm milk and crushed aspirin, down in a cosy specially made up bed in the barn. I pled for her to be brought indoors, or at least be allowed into the shed where she and her great friend Fluffy slept, sharing their kittens, both nursing the lucky survivor left from each litter to keep the cats content and a home always found. The rest of the litter disappeared like magic and was never talked about. Quarantine was not explained and a vet was never considered, but no other cat suffered a similar fate and in time the black and white cat was back in the fold, having fully recovered despite her advancing years.

One of our neighbours who owned a black milking cow had a beautiful well-rounded collie with a curly coal-black coat. Both the dog and the cow shone like polished jet in the sunshine as they made their way along the sheep walks in the hills behind the houses heading for different pastures. We loved the dog and found Jimmy Oag an affable fellow, indeed, how could you not like a man who called his dog Tworky!

Looking back, it seems as if the most popular first names in the village were Dolly and Jimmy, and with Mackay being the dominant surname, bye-names were used as a necessary identification rather than a medium for insult.

31

However, many were just that and we children were well warned of the hell-fire and damnation that would rain down upon us if we dared to use a derogatory tag. Which we did, and suffered for it, but often as not it was well worth the risk.

To ensure we had a healthy respect for dogs we had Sporran living next door, a short-legged, black, and alarmingly grumpy, low-slung creature whose bark was every bit as bad as his bite. He was probably a Dachshund. We were welcomed into every home in the village and made occasional raids on neighbours for one reason or another during the course of our play, but Sporran's bad nature kept us away from Etta and Jimmy's, except for the odd occasion when curiosity, or necessity, drove us to their fireside. Jimmy liked to entice us to stroke Sporran to the accompaniment of snarls through curled back lips and flashing white teeth, and Etta's, 'Tich, tich, Jimmy. Can't you leave the children alone.'

'Sporran would never harm them, as gentle as a lamb,' Jimmy replied, nursing this ferocious beast and daring us to risk the gnashing teeth but only the bravest, or the stupidest, did. The spectacle in itself kept us away for weeks, until temptation took us back again.

I had good reason to hate that dog. He killed my cousin Pat's young cat left in our care when her family holidayed. And it was Sporran too who was suspected of taking a chunk out of the side of Snowball, our only tomcat, and a cat I fought for before he met this grizzly fate. Dad was at home when I asked what could be wrong with Snowball who had refused to leap down from the windowsill where he sat meowing in at our family sitting round the breakfast table.

As usual, nobody took heed of me or the cat so the minute the meal was over I rushed out and reached up for him. The cat howled. I quickly drew back my hands to discover one was covered in blood. Then I howled, louder than the cat. There was a gaping hole in his side. My father examined Snowball asking me to hold him while he, whose Naval training

32

equipped him for such emergencies, took out his ditty box where instruments of torture lay. I knew because he had stitched a gash in my hand after I fell on the long and highly dangerous ice run we made in the hills one very hard winter, scattered with shards as sharp as broken glass.

'Stand still, Lassie,' was the only sympathy I got, but the memory is still as colourful as the woollen pixie hats we wore tied under our chins with long pleated ropes of wool. Mittens were either lost or so caked in snow they were kept in our pockets while we sucked our frozen fingers back into agonizing life.

Now as he sterilised the needle and gut, painstakingly stitching up the cat I was commissioned to supress any attempt to resist the needle while I quietly sobbed into my pet's blood-spattered fur. Physically, Snowball recovered well, Dad very proud of his needlework, but the cat was never the same again and about a year later disappeared. I mourned his loss and was never told the source of it until long after when my brother Neil chose to enlighten me. There being no such thing as a cat litter tray in our youth, when Snowball committed the cardinal sin of using hidden reaches of the house rather than go outside to the toilet, he was quietly removed from our lives, with anyone in the know well warned, 'Do not tell Joan.' One likes to think there would be a better understanding of a cat's needs today.

My pal, Hamie Lad, as I called him, had a passionate liking for Snowball, playing with him when the weather opposed our mothers' need to see us out from under their feet. The kitten's unusual short haired, all white coat with this big black splodge right in the middle of his forehead, along with being a boy cat, made him something to boast of! One day he went missing, nowhere to be found. Later I went to find Hamish who had not been seen either that same day. There, curled up on their blue sofa was my kitten, sound asleep. Old Papa was in his habitual chair by the fire, grizzled head bent over his creels as he made a complicated repair. Hamish was defiant that he had been given the kitten, backed by his mother who had no reason to believe otherwise. I was appalled at this turn of affairs.

I hung about their snug living room, under the eaves of the only habitable thatched home left in the village, scuffing my feet in misery, stroking a kitten that seemed perfectly happy with his new home. I was not happy. Watching carefully, and when every back was turned, I slipped my hand over the kitten and stuffed him up my jumper. As I began to back out the permanently open door, Maggie turned from the doorstep slices of bread she habitually cut for any child to hand, slathering them with sweet condensed milk over a thick spread of butter.

'Wait for your piece, Joan.' Maggie offered this special treat before catching the look of terror on my face. I was ready for full flight, kitten tightly held under its woolly disguise.

Papa only bothered with our raucous play to demand an instant, 'Wheest!' the minute he turned his ear to the whistling, spitting wireless as he moved the knob towards the Home Service for the daily news. Hamish's attention was focused on the mouth-watering piece about to be placed in his outstretched hand.

Instead, his mother dropped the breadknife, tipped her head to one side and quizzically demanded, 'What have you got under your jumper, Joan?' I spun round and took off out her door like a rabbit at the first sound of a shot-gun.

To this day, I remember the horror of how it felt to steal. It was my kitten and Hamish was the one who took it, but for me to spirit it out of the house against the matriarchal authority that governed so much of our lives was stealing, and by the time I reached our gate, Maggie Bell was hot on my heels. I fled into the safety of our house and hid in the pantry, the kitten still clutched under my Fair Isle patterned jumper. Such was my horror, anything that reminded me of that day was shunned. Regardless of fashion, I never put Fair Isle on my back again, making sure the jumper was fatally holed soon after.

Maggie, panting in the door, shouted, 'Marion,' as my mother appeared from the scullery wondering what the to-do was about. 'What on earth is wrong with Joan? She's run away with Hamish's new kitten and he'll be heart broken.' My knees began to shake as two irate mothers defended the characters of their children. I crept out, leaving the kitten in the dark recess of that well-stocked cupboard.

Between sobs I swore I never gave the kitten away and my hysterical imploring was believed. Poor Maggie, who had lost the battle to my indignant mother, patted my head and rubbing my tears away with the corner of her overall went home to deal with her recalcitrant son.

'Oh, *Mo Gaol*, what would make him do that?' and with a heavy sigh, she went out the door. Love of the cat, I could have told her, but I was too mean-spirited to allow him keep the cherished kitten. I had a long way to go in life's lessons and so, no doubt, had Hamish.

As with most disagreements between children, there was no more said about it, but the next time Hamish made his way down the road I took a leaf out of the black and white cat's book and went tearing up to meet him, temper flaring. There was no standoff. I flew at him with feet and fists, and he ably defended himself, fisticuffs often being the way we ended our disputes, with no parental interference. But his friendship had its advantages. After we both headed for the primary school in Bettyhill, the Kirtomy school deemed no longer necessary for educating the village children not long before we reached school-age, I was the only girl always chosen for the scratch football teams, courtesy of my friend Hamish whose skills learned on the hills of Kirtomy put him at the head of the team every time. And I was his crack goalie.

Chapter 4

'Cats and monkeys; monkeys and cats;
all human life is there.'

Henry James

Monkey Business

Another favourite canine was Swannie, that much loved dog of our early years who could play a mean game of hide-and-seek but a great disappointment in goals, a position she was obliged to take as Hamish and I played against each other, vying to get the ball past Swannie. She was the smooth-haired black and white collie bitch belonging to Merran who lived a solitary life in the half-house down from our own home. No doubt the field that separated most houses was as much a blessing for her as it was to us. This often cantankerous old woman caused children no end of trouble and we delighted in calling her The Witch. But we loved Swannie, despite our on/off relationship with Merran who treated Swannie more as a companion than a working dog. She had one milking cow, housed in a thatched low-roofed byre behind her home.

Thinking back I remember glorious early morning sunshine, sleepily rubbing my eyes, lying in bed listening to Merran's screeching voice as she passed through the village, herding her red cow towards the iron-gate to find fresh pastures outside the encircling fence that protected the village from marauding animals. Bringing back her cow in the evening, she continued to stridently call upon Swannie to assist its passage.

Occasionally, the driver of one of the few cars entering the village opened the gate to gain access, then shirked closing it. Merran's cow was an opportunist and would make its leisurely way home, munching at the long grass in the

36

ditches that edged the road. Sandra, my older sister, another opportunist, squirted the warm milk into our open mouths, or into one of the jam jars we used to collect bees, for the pleasure of scrutinising their behaviour before releasing them. Occasionally, mischief got the better of us and a bee would be brought back to our mother and thrust in front of her nose as it danced and buzzed angrily in its enforced captivity. We believed it to be the only thing in the whole wide world that terrified her. Sometimes her screaming could be heard a mile away if one dared to buzz round her head as she hung out the washing, or went on the long walk to fetch pails of drinking and cooking water from the well.

My mother always welcomed Merran on her daily visits but her expression changed at the all too often sight of the old woman approaching, hands clasped behind her back, head bent forward, muttering underneath her breath and slowly shaking her head. It meant trouble for one of us. It never stopped us running in and out of her house at will, to sit at her meagre fire in the inglenook of her tiny kitchen and listen to her tales. Invariably, a soot-black pot or kettle would hang from the sway ensuring some of the curling smoke filtered into the room rather than up the chimney, but it was a clean and tidy room, and she was a clean and tidy woman.

Not like Ishby, another old woman who lived at the far end of the Overside, an area banned to us. The children suspected she was a real witch, but we liked her, so never called her a witch. Her hands were as black as a mole's, as was the little button rose that snuffled out above a dark moustache. Her face was round and kindly, and when we defied authority and visited her, heart in mouth, hoping to see her black cat, or maybe her broomstick, she gave us a kindly welcome. She had the shape, snuffle and shuffle of Mrs Tiggy-Winkle. Our parents banned us in case we bothered her. She had her own way of getting at any who bothered her. She had the second sight, and the ability to read a tea cup, with considerable

37

accuracy too! Her readings could put the fear of death into any bold enough to risk a cup of her tea, the risk being to the stomach more than the mind.

It was Merran's we gravitated towards with no fear of contamination or black cats. Hers was one of the few homes without a cat. Two straight-backed, plain wooden chairs graced each side of the fire, her own on the left as hard seated as the chair for a visitor. We would be invited to sit on the right, with neither arms nor cushions on either chair to aid comfort. To the best of my recollection the floor was of Caithness flagstone and relieved only on a Sunday with a colourful rag rug, taken out for ornamental purposes, being safe from fireside spills as no cooking was carried out on a Sunday. Sunday was for church, walking the three miles there and back, and for bible reading. There was a faded red velvet chaise longue set against the back wall, opposite a small square table in front of the tiny window with a well-worn waxed cloth – I'm certain it was green with cream squares – and a tall dresser on the wall opposite the fireside containing much of Merran's crockery.

We were never turned from her door but this did not stop her from taking our mothers to task at our many misdemeanours. Each New Year she took from the dresser a bottle of ginger wine to give each of us a tiny glass of the warming syrupy drink. We loved it! And in that cupboard too she would have a bottle of port, for that would be the drink she would offer each caller, served in tiny glasses, for the men would always pay her a visit, not on Hogmanay, but on New Year's Day, it being traditional in Kirtomy to celebrate New Year on that day.

In the spring and summer, with a guile beyond our years, we took off to the braes by the side of the burn to pick posies of primroses for Merran, to make up for some trivial offence hoping the offering would prevent the wrong reaching authoritative ears. We knew she loved those wild flowers and would be mollified...for a while. But there was always the possibility of retribution to keep an edge on our anxiety when empty bellies drove us home to every meal with an inbuilt accuracy thwarted only when so engrossed in our adventures we lost even the need to eat, the day ending in tears when strident shouts did not reach us and a searcher eventually traced our wandering footsteps whether en route home or still focused on our fun. Snacks were never doled out, apart from Maggie Bell's condensed milk pieces, the urgency of our hunger well satisfied with good plain cooking when we eventually got home. Food was never denied as a punishment.

Merran had a soft spot for Magnus, the first boy born into our family, calling him Nena's Bowey, but there was a dubious relationship with Neil, the youngest child. We would meet our mother, an exasperated look on her face. 'Where is that wringing devil now? Just wait till I get my hands on him!' I never worked out why we were wringing, apart from when wet, but then, it may have been 'ringing', either as confusing as the other, but we accepted all invectives without question.

He and I had much in common, both loving animals and it was he who brought the first dog into our household. By then, Sandra and I were teenagers and Neil was in the primary school along with Muriel and Magnus, where they roamed at will despite being warned to stay within the confines of the school playground. Confinement was not a familiar concept to the children of Kirtomy.

On one of these ventures, Neil and his pal came across a man going to drown puppies. They were fat, cuddly, sand-coloured creatures, squirming in delight when the boys asked to hold them; irresistible. The inevitable result – two of the puppies were spirited into the boys' outdoor toilets. At play time, Neil commanded a whip-round to buy biscuits at the local shop for the hungry puppies. It was this coercion of funds from other pupils that earned him yet another severe belting from the headmaster when his constant need to go to the toilet, with other children getting in on the act, ended in the discovery of the puppies.

'You can't have that puppy, Neil,' our mother warned when he arrived home with his new best friend, pleading to keep the small, bear-like creature.

'You'll take him back tomorrow,' she insisted.

'He'll be drowned!' This was well backed up by Muriel who was three years his senior, and Magnus a year older than her. Against such odds, my mother caved in, on the understanding the pup came from small stock, thinking that would be manageable. Knowing he could get the puppy on that strict condition, Neil pestered every day to know what was the yardstick and in desperation was told, 'Not any bigger than the arm of the couch.' So started a daily measurement of the growing dog, Neill pressing down on his rump and seriously warning Brandy not to grow bigger. When the dog's ears appeared above the low-slung arm, he avowed, 'You said his head.' And when that defied advice and quickly shot above the couch, it was 'You said his shoulders.'

Eventually it dawned that Brandy was a much loved member of the family. Tactics changed and the dog was encourage to grow bigger, Neil lifting him under his ribcage to ensure he was now well above the yardstick. He was a big solid lump of a dog that belied Neil's constant assurances his mother was a Corgi to compensate for the fact we were well informed the puppy's father was an Alsatian. It would have been a union worth the watching but Brandy hadn't an aggressive bone in his russet coloured body so his guard dog pedigree gave no cause for concern. In fact, he was an extremely good dog and only misbehaved when he got in tow with the dog I defied all logic to have and to hold, not long after my marriage when my mother's terrier gave birth to puppies. Another idea that seemed so good at the time.

Brandy grew into old age long after Neil left Kirtomy at the age of 11 to attend the Sutherland Technical School, boarding there, only allowed home during holidays, a far cry from later years when pupils were bussed home every weekend. Afterwards he joined the Merchant Navy seeing little of his dog but usurping him with a monkey that caused no end of trouble when his ship came back to Southampton for scrapping. He swears he walked out of the docks with the monkey sitting on his shoulder, not being aware of the hue and cry that went out all across the land when it dawned that a suspect species had been 'smuggled' into the country.

Our first knowledge came when a uniformed policeman walked up the path to the front door in Kirtomy demanding of our mother Neil's whereabouts. For a woman who had every respect for the law, being told the police were seeking her son from the shores of the south coast to the cliffs of the north, horrified her. Neil seldom came straight home as he had many friends to call on especially in London where he initially headed, monkey as a side-kick fully made up with pub crawling and train travel. Neil's intention was to bring his ship mate north, after a bit of a holiday in the south, and see if I, who had got him out of other scrapes with animals, would look after his monkey until he got another ship. During the time it took me to trace him, the only good thing that came out of this monkey business was our mother's loss of weight, something she had been attempting with little success, the pantry stuffed with boxes of Energene Rolls that we children loved to pinch, for the pleasure of having them dissolve in our mouths without putting a tooth near them.

'What possessed you to think we could look after a monkey, anyway?' I asked, long after our telephone conversation that saw him heading with his monkey still on his shoulder, to the nearest police station.

Nobody could be angry as he was heartbroken because the monkey was put to sleep, but I sighed in recognition when he shrugged his shoulders and said, 'It seemed a good idea at the time.'

Chapter 5

*'Noise proves nothing. Often a hen who has merely laid
an egg cackles as if she had laid an asteroid.'*

Mark Twain

The Crowing Hen

Recollection of the dogs from my childhood is strong,
but what of the cats. The curious thing is, I have no memory of
any feral cats roaming the village. Almost every house had a
cat, some two, and of course, the children were allowed cats for
pets, not dogs or rabbits, and a horse for personal gratification
was unheard of, although our barn stored a wonderful saddle,
belonging to a grand-aunt of yesteryear who lived in the next-
door village of Armadale. Apparently she was a tall, elegant
woman, considered to be very handsome and rode about the
area side-saddle in a dark green riding habit, much to the
admiration of her peers. The saddle lay there for years but was
gone by the time I shocked the Melvich community by taking
into its midst the first recreational equines since years gone by
when the last of the working Clydesdales vanished from our
area. That was near 40 years ago and there's been horses and
ponies in the village ever since!

Our home in Kirtomy has excellent outbuildings, a
shed where the cats had their kittens and from where my
mother did her massive washings close to an outside fire for
boiling water, and of course, the whites, that being of great
personal pride to her. I once asked, 'What gives you the most
pleasure to see,' and she answered, 'A line full of white
washing billowing in the breeze.' To achieve this, she not only

had to lug the washing to the shed, build a fire and gather the fuel, but she also had to fetch the water from either the barrel at the bottom of the row of outbuildings involving a long trip back down to the foot of the garden. When a dry spell came, all domestic as well as drinking water had to come from the well which was a good way off, over the perimeter dyke at the back and on up a small hill before a trek to the well which served several households. The three long washing lines were way down the back of the house in a flat area that commanded some wonderful see breezes, or a howling gale, but little interfered with the Monday wash and the need to get it dried, ironed and aired, so you can understand her pride in achieving this along with the many other tasks of the day. Feeding the opportunist cats who were expected to hunt for most of their food, was low on her agenda, scraps rather than specially selected tins of cat food keeping them healthy, sleek and disease-free.

Attached to the shed is the byre which in the early days before water was piped to the village, housed the family lavatory, a large wooden affair, single occupancy, thank goodness, and I'm merciful too that my memory of its use retains no odious flashbacks. On the other side of the byre we had the stable, a place of far greater interest, as was the barn next door, all under one long red roof. This sturdy row of stone buildings, so necessary in our grandfather's day when the croft was in full use, lay a short distance from the house and once a year, in the spring, Jimmy Clachan arrived with his big working Clydesdale, having walked him all the way from Bettyhill to carry out the village ploughing and, joy of joys, stable this seemingly placid, though not always predictable, animal with us for as many nights as the job required. The other night, I watched a TV programme where the presenters had travelled to remote areas of China and were quite taken aback that poverty was such that two villages shared the one donkey. I don't know how many villages shared Jimmy Clachan's Clydesdale, but nobody cried poverty.

Other than the cats' use of the shed, the Clydesdale's use of the stable, and Swannie's use of the barn when Merran caused no end of speculation by taking a trip to Canada leaving her dog with my mother, we had no animals there or on the croft land allocated to the house except for the ubiquitous hens watched over by a triumphant rooster, housed in a white rather copious building attached to the main house with its dark red door and small hatchway to allow hens in and out to their nesting boxes. They shared this house with two ducks, a beautiful glossy metallic black, Sandra's pet, and a skinny dull khaki coloured duck that was undoubtedly mine. They were the best of mates as were Sandra and I as we grew up.

We did however, have one particular hen that much preferred to lay her egg in the centre of Magnus's bed in the well plumped up feather quilts of that time. Our mother would put a finger to her mouth and say, 'Sssh! Listen.' We could then hear the slight creak as this Rhode Island Red very cautiously crept her way upstairs, stopping and listening every other step. We held our breath. It wasn't long before a loud squawk, then boastful cackles before rising to a crescendo that came dangerously close to the proverbial crowing hen as she rushed back down stairs, job done! She never made a mess and it never ceased to amuse, her egg always considered a special treat usually ending up in the plastic blue or pink cockerel-shaped egg-cups belonging to Muriel and Magnus, with much arguing as to who had the previous egg. I was all of three years older and considered past such indulgences and Neil too small then to get his tuppence-worth into the debate. When he found his voice, he made up for being the last to enter into the world in what was known as the Far-Off bedroom, with its front window facing across the valley, another to the south trapping whatever sun shone, and always a cosy fire in the hearth when there was a new baby ensconced with our mother

44

in the big, wooden-ended bed where a district nurse would often be found, quietly gossiping with our mother over the rail of baby clothes airing in front of the peat fire.

With our father away at sea most of the time, he saw no need to nurture the land, other than grow tatties, a task seen to by our extremely able mother who saw also to our upbringing, instilling principles that gave him great peace of mind and a quiet pride in his brood. I never once remember her having to threaten, 'Wait till your father comes home.' Her authority had no need, but the very thought of being brought to task by our father kept us on our toes. Not that I ever saw him raise a hand in anger at what he always referred to as 'lassies'; it was his disappointment that made us think twice. Mind you, Nena's Boey drove her to go direct to our father one day and Magnus was removed from our sight to be dealt with. I don't recall the crime that required immediate retribution, just the shock that our father had had enough and was taking action. As for Neil, who was exceptionally mischievous, his need to be taken aside by our father caused little alarm as its frequency rendered the act less offensive, and no doubt, less effective.

Except for one memorable occasion. With unbelievable determination, Neil cornered our father and sprayed a fully-charged large water pistol all over him, then shot out the door with Dad straight after him, wiping the drenching water from his shocked face. Instead of taking off, Neil hid and with a replenished weapon let fire again. By now he was being chased all around the house. He then completely disappeared. At meal time he was not to be found. Alarm bells began to ring and the search went out. Someone said they were certain he'd gone into Merran's.

'I'll go myself,' his father said with unaccustomed grimness. Merran assured him Neil had not been over her door that day. Time passed with no Neil to be found. However, an unusual noise alerted the old woman to the fact that someone was in her house. Rather than accost the miscreant herself, she stood in her doorway and hailed a passer-by to tell Dad to come back and renew the search. There, up her narrow stair, Neil was found, hiding under her bed, a place none of us dared to set foot, despite our inquisitive desire to know what The Witch kept up there. Even some adults said that's where she kept her broomstick.

Dragged out and made to answer for his misbehaviour, he was well advised, 'You make sure you go back down there tomorrow, straight after school, and tell Merran how sorry you are for your behaviour.' Being a Sunday evening, Dad set off for Scrabster, the port he sailed from, and me with him as by then I was attending Miller Academy in Thurso, staying with the Grant family during the week.

Neil had a whole day to think about it while his siblings delighted in adding weight to his anxiety by tempting, 'She'll turn you into a frog for going up her stairs.'

That afternoon, in fact the minute his school bag got its usual hurl onto the couch, down the road he went, returning ages later with a big grin on his face. We thought it an end to the matter. It was the next morning before Merran made her head-shaking, hands clasped behind her back, way up by the outhouses, past the henhouse and through the side gate. Our mother took in her demeanour as she passed the front window, and sighed heavily.

'What did he do now?' she asked, desperate to get on with the washing.

'Do you know what he did, that boy?' My mother inclined her head in a questioning manner, knowing nothing, but fearing much.

'He came into my house and said his father told him he was to apologise for hiding under my bed, she nodded, spittle gathering at the corners of her mouth. My mother knew when to keep quiet. It was a well-known scenario and she needed more information before she could open her mouth.

'Hiding in my bedroom was bad enough.' This required contemplative silence, followed by an outraged, 'Taking the Lord's name into his outrageous behaviour…'

'He went straight down to see you the minute he came home, to say sorry. He was so long with you I had to keep his food hot for him,' my mother interrupted the tirade, wondering what on earth was to come next.

'Magnus,' Merran emphasised, referring to our father for whom she had great respect, 'said Neil would be back to apologise and I thought that was what took him back over my door. I asked him to sit down. Do you know what he did?' Her voice rose to a crescendo. My mother's heart began to hammer in anticipation. What could he have done to cause such indignation?

'He said he would rather get down on his knees!' the old woman screeched.

'He was very sorry,' said my mother, thinking, so well he should have been with the row he got for doing such an outrageous thing as go up Merran's stair, leave alone hide under her bed all Sunday afternoon. He told us later he listened to Merran's long readings of the Bible and her lengthy prayers, the quiet Swannie her only convert and Neil praying she would go out until he could escape.

'Sorry!' screamed the old woman. 'Sorry! You think he was sorry. Not him. He got down on his knees and prayed that the good Lord would forgive me. Me! For all the trouble I cause him. He even said, if I asked for deliverance, he was sure God would give it to me.'

By now she was spitting with righteous anger and my poor mother, regardless of any annoyance at her young son, had difficulty in keeping a straight face. It was she rather than Neil who told me the sorry tale, when, on the following Friday after my return home, I pulled from my schoolbag, the white and pink sugar mice I always bought for him out of the generous pocket money she gave me. He was not to have

47

them. He was still paying for his belief that Merran could be changed by divine intervention and his life would be made easier.

I remember once saying to my mother, 'Neil was spoiled.' 'Yes,' she agreed, 'and we know who spoiled him!' He was seven years my junior, he had many of my own personality traits and even when I left the same technical college he would attend, after taking a business course and took up employment at the Atomic Station, a bus ride away at Dounreay, coming home in the evenings, he would often greet me with, 'Will you come out and play Cowboys and Indians with me?' And sometimes I did!

When left at times in charge of my three younger siblings, both Muriel and Magnus who were closer than twins, often accused me of acting for the instigator of the fight, rather than defending their innocent stance. It was probably during those formative years I learned the art of diplomacy in an attempt to keep the peace I always loved.

Even as a small child, I could not abide the thought of corporal punishment and when Sandra did the unthinkable, going without permission to the shore, where the memory of a young boy's drowning meant strict vigilance. Our mother's long and frantic search ended in Sandra being taken into the room, that cold highly polished sitting room, used only for special occasions and the rare administration of punishment. As my mother exercised her right hand with more power than was usual, I stuck into her, walloping her legs as hard as my small form could drive, screaming, 'Leave Sandra alone, leave her alone.' This intervention stayed her hand and nothing of it appeared to come to our father's ears. Once the punishment was doled out, we never heard more of our offences, nor did a sore backside last much longer than the next five minutes.

We were used to Jimmy's Clydesdale horse with his rich dark brown coat, but were always warned not to go near the horse on our own. However, this great creature must have had a degree of tolerance with us children constantly begging for rides on his back. We knew that when stripped of his working harness and left to his own devices to graze the steep brae that dropped to a plateau bordering the burn that cut Kirtomy in half, the warning would be issued again, 'Don't go anywhere near that horse when Jimmy's not with him.'

Sandra and I took great delight in bringing our cousin Joan, home on holiday from Glasgow, to the field at the foot of that brae to shout and tease the horse peacefully minding his own business scratching his great big backside on the fence at the top. It was a game of dare, playing Chicken with a horse. It never took much to make him stampede down the hill while we waited, daring each other until the last minute, then race in terror to climb the dyke and over the wire fence bolted onto its top before the horse could get his teeth into our fleeing rear ends. Many a frock had to find alternative reasons for its tear as we skimmed the barbed wire. But that day, with Joan not quite so nimble on her feet as her country cousins, we barely made it, and being found out ensured our behinds were a lot sorer than had the horse got a nip at us rather than our mother's strong right hand.

Not that Joan told, she had a brother of her own and was well aware of the penalties of being a tell-tale-tit. We trooped back home, happy with our fun, our cousin's tears all dried up, hungry for the tea that would be all the more sumptious with visitors to please.

'What's wrong with that child that she can't sit still for two minutes,' was cast in my direction, but soon it was obvious all three of us were furiously scratching. Investigation proved we were covered in ticks to the absolute horror of Joan's mother, a fastidious woman who passed her dainty form on to her daughter, whereas her husband, my mother's brother, was a big, generous man who laughed a lot. In demanding where we spent the afternoon to identify the source of the ticks, the story came out and so Sandra and I suffered for our pleasures. Sandra, being three years older, probably suffered the more for her seniority and in truth, though not quite the tom-boy I was, she had an inbuilt source of courage that baulked at nothing whereas I was more reticent when it came to obvious danger.

Writing about the horses, I remember when I got a tanned backside I felt quite unfair over another horse attempting to take a serious chunk out of my behind while fleeing over a dyke, and it was not Jimmy Clachan's Clydesdale, whoever else the animal belonged to. We often took shortcuts through fields as we raced from school in Bettyhill to the homes of friends, to the shop, or to play in the woods nearby, despite being told not to. This day I went with Doris Mackenzie to her home and we were late in setting off back to school. 'You'll just have to suffer the consequences. Don't take the shortcut, because that horse will chase you,' we were well warned before setting off.

'We'll have to,' Doris whispered. 'We can run faster than him.' She could maybe, she was older with even longer legs than I and was half way through the field before it dawned on the horse. He caught up with me and made a grab just as I shot over the dyke. My initial howl was of terror, but hearing the rip in my kilt I yelled even louder. Annie Nicol, who lived close by came out to see what all the fuss was about.

'You should never have been in there with that horse,' she admonished wondering if the horse had hurt me.

'No,' I sobbed 'He tore my kilt and my mother will kill me.' Kilts were expensive even then and it had been a day for a school photo, me sent out in my best and warned, do not get dirty and do not lose your hair ribbon, both of which I managed to achieve until after the photo was taken. But going home with a torn kilt was beyond my allocation of courage.

However, my day was saved, except for a severe telling off for being late, Doris having made it in time and avowing no knowledge of where I had got to. Mrs Nicol sewed the kilt while I stood there in my knickers, mortified. At least they were my own knickers. Another time I strayed from the playing field, fell into a burn, up to my neck and was frog marched to the Headmaster's house to be kitted out in clothes belonging to his wife, not a big woman, but I was only six and her bloomers swamped me. I spent the rest of the day trying to ensure their long elasticated legs did not come down below my knees, where her son's shirt hem stopped, acting reasonably well as a dress.

It was some time afterwards when the kilt was donned again that retribution caught up with me when my mother spotted the repair. A full explanation was demanded. 'You had no right to tell anyone I would kill you for tearing your clothes,' she scolded and walloped to emphasise her point, insisting the anger had nothing to do with the beautifully repaired kilt, but that I would dare to say I was afraid of being killed. 'If you ever say the likes of that again to anyone, I'll kill you!' She didn't even realise the worth of her threat, and one of us would be threatened with annihilation at least once a day! But we knew exactly what was meant, so my best ploy, if I wanted to live, was to stay well away from horses.

I would never have believed that in times to come, I would have horses as part of my life for close on 30 years. And there were few more interested in their welfare than my mother!

Chapter 6

'If man could be crossed with a cat, it would improve man but deteriorate the cat.'

T. S. Eliot

So Many Cats

It was cats that held my attention. I viewed each one that came into the household as mine, other than the black and white cat. She remained aloof to all but our father and knew every time he was due to arrive home. Sitting on the dyke that bordered the front garden, patiently waiting his arrival for at least an hour before he appeared, she would follow him into the house and whenever he sat in an armchair, take up residence upon the arm, her stance regal, front paws tucked neatly under a proudly jutting white chest, black tail curled round dainty white feet, contentment radiating from a face that gave me my first insight into the intensity of a cat's stare. No other cat had the mien of the black and white cat, repelling any expectation of kittenish behaviour, quite the antithesis of her companion, Fluffy. How did she know, long before his weekly appearance that my father would arrive that day, around that time? The fact he carried a big tray with a fry of the most delectable fish may have had an influence as the cats loved raw fish and pestered for their share the minute our mother took out the big filleting knife. Yet, she was always there, patiently awaiting his arrival from the port of Scrabster, all of 30 miles away. Thirty miles in the late forties was not a distance to take lightly.

During her lifetime I was allowed a long-haired light and dark brown striped kitten I called Fluffy. We weren't very imaginative when it came to the naming of cats but despite that, Fluffy and the black and white cat became firm friends. Neither was neutered, no more than any other female cat in the village. If a vet had to be called, it would be to attend sheep or cattle and then only after long and hard deliberation. The crofters knew how to deal with tasks today considered needful of a trip to the vet or a call out. There were neither tags nor paper identifications, passports nor stocking numbers to keep tabs on both the crofters and their stock. I don't suppose there were subsidies either, any government largesse would go to the landlords, not the tenants. To ask a vet to attend a cat was unheard of, indeed, it would be many years into the future before the area sustained a small animal practice in the town of Thurso, with a fleet of vets seeing to agricultural requirements as well as a variety of small animals unbeknown then to the likes of Kirtomy. Folks were bemused enough when Jimmy and Etta's daughter-in-law walked about with a tiny dog tucked under her arm, bushy tail curled up at one end and a squashed in face at the other denying the possibility of it being a squirrel, not that we knew much of squirrels either.

The usual route for a male kitten was drowning at birth or being swiftly removed from their bits by certain males known for their skills with the knife, faster than a vet can now administers an injection, so much care is taken of the animal's wellfare, and a good thing too. It wasn't unusual for a strange tom to arrive from a distant village to have it off with the local good-time girls, and then, after he did his bit to serve the community, he'd oblige by disappearing back home. At least that's what we were told, but thinking back, I wonder the fate of these wandering Lotharios.

There was no doubt queens were preferable to toms and kittens were rigorously inspected so no error was made. My cousin Pat's household was a haven for children and pets, and always a cat about. Her daughter, Hazel, when quite small, was found one day with a little black kitten held upside down

53

in her hands while the mother howled round the child's feet demanding her offspring back. Hazel was intent upon examining the squirming kitten, a big frown on her face.

'What are you doing with that kitten, Hazel?' her mother demanded, coming to the rescue.

'Am's looking for him's toms,' she indignantly replied. And so the young learn!

It was weird how Fluffy and the black and white cat often kittened together, in the shed. They were allowed to keep one offspring, though sometimes two, according to needs, and without rancour, both mothers nursed the lucky survivor, sharing the feeding, grooming, and occasional bringing of wrath upon their heads when met by our mother, making their way up to the house with a kitten firmly gripped by the scruff of its neck, speed essential if they were to achieve their goal of a cosy nook in the house. My first experience of this feline behaviour had me flying to the house convinced I had witnessed an atrocity.

'The cat is eating its kitten.' I gasped, sick with the horror of it all.

'Don't be ridiculous,' I was told while the cat was soundly rebuked and sent packing back to the shed. Despite this constant need to introduce their progeny to the house, my mother insisted they remain in their nest, in a big zinc bath, once the receptacle of our weekly grime, hauled in front of a huge fire and filled with hot water from a small reservoir on the side of the hot range, or the kettle hissing steam on its black burnished top. The bath doubled its use when the washing board was plunged into its steaming soapy depth on a Monday morning, down at the shed where the weekly wash was dealt with. Wear and tear eventually took its toll and a leak relegated it fit only for the cats, filled with old woolly sweaters, brightest of all no doubt, my abandoned Fair Isle jumper, though Muriel fell heir to most of my clothes first, nothing abandoned to the shed until thoroughly worn, or damaged beyond use!

The shed housed a large mangle, or wringer as we knew it, with rollers fit to handle the large woollen blankets washed every Spring, and it was into that monstrous contraption Sandra fed our first doll. It was two headed, one black, the other white, brought to us from foreign shores by our father. Each was a fine looking doll in its own right, stunningly dressed, a long colourful satin striped gown worn by the dusky maiden covering the blonde head, and when you put your hand under the skirts and flicked her over, a rush of delicate froth hid the dark-skinned lady with her black curls and big smile to give you a fair complexioned damsel of exquisite taste in gowns. The doll was greatly admired by the grown-ups who had no compunction about sticking their hands under her skirts and finding a head, rather than legs! It may well have been for that reason the doll met its grizzly fate.

Sandra had a lot of time for a sister more than three years her junior and all my young years she included me in her activities, so it wasn't a one off when I was persuaded to turn the handle while she fed the doll in all its glory, black cloth head first, into a wringer with jaws that could be adjusted to take the thick blankets. I have better recollection of the act than the aftermath so she, no doubt, absorbed the consequences of such a wayward act. We were never given another doll, nor did we grieve for one, unlike Muriel who had a passion for her dolls and bought with the first money she ever earned, a three foot doll for Sandra's first born girl, Lorna. Lorna loved that doll and wheeling it through Bettyhill one day, with the triplets in tow, a passer-by was intrigued and wanted to know all their names, believing the child in the buggy to be as real as the girls, much to their amusement.

There were times when the cats spirited away their entire litters before our mother could bring her adjudication into effect, and foolish children, we never split on their hideaways, not realising that by the time they brought their kittens back into the fold, it was the worse for all concerned.

Nor did we ever take into consideration the distress such primitive methods of disposal caused our mother each time she had to do this loathsome task. It caused many bad memories for at times a child could not be left to its own devices, and the act had to be carried out with howling child in tow. The children were told never to play in the burn below the bridge, nightmares brought on by warnings of the bottomless pools and whirlpools that lay in its depth as the brown peaty water rushed towards the sea. Of course, we disobeyed that rule as we did others and to our horror discovered that below the bridge in the deeper pools many a new born litter met its fate. This discovery made once, assured you never again poked about or opened any old lisle stocking that was caught by a stone; you got a stick and assisted it on its way, wiping away tears with the hem of your cotton frock. Water born adventures were always spring and summer activities usually bringing about hours of contented play.

More bad memories stem from the times a kitten was slow to grasp the niceties of family living and none noticing its desperate scrabbling seeking some part of the floor that yielded to its need to scrape a hole. The poor creature's punishment of having its nose rubbed into its newly formed toilet was met with my howls of derision on the kitten's behalf when I could not reach it in time to rush it out the door and away from such harsh training methods. I found this disturbingly unacceptable. Not for one moment did our parents believe this to be cruel. Cats had to be clean, and being clean meant a clear demand to be let out when needs must, or save their needs for the nocturnal hours which were never spent in the house, unless by default, and that did not end well, a tired mother not amused to get up in the middle of the night to let out a howling cat. A litter tray was never heard of, nor was a catflap!

'If that kitten doesn't ask out, you can't keep her. She'll soon learn,' and that was an end to the matter. Quite different from later life at The Sheiling Guest House and my own method of training that left one of our cats with a rather peculiar habit. When Smudge had her litter of four kittens, no matter how busy the kitchen with guests, friends or family, the second anyone spotted a kitten looking stressed, the shout when up, 'Grab the kittens!'

To the astonishment of any guest who happened to come it to enjoy the spectacle of a playful mother with her little brood romping about the feet of a house rabbit, I would snatch up two kittens, rush out to the back green and plonk them down on the grass. There they sat waiting until I, or Katrina who was by then expecting our first grandchild, placed the other two kittens down beside them. Then, in unison, they would all raise their tails, checking to see all were at the ready, then tails would quiver while they piddled into the grass. It was an amusing scene, watching this row of vibrating tails and kittens checking with each other to make sure they were all performing as expected.

The peculiarity became evident when The Hobbit, our first ever boy cat, did not grow out of this habit and waited patiently for his sister, Poodie-Pooh to join him on the back green, until eventually she told him to grow up and stop embarrassing her because from now on, her ablutions were to be carried out in private. But for as long as he lived, and he lived a long time, growing into a big handsome tom, he sat in the grass to pee, with tail waving like a beacon, looking around him as if he were seeking out his siblings to ensure all was as it should be.

We kept two from the litter, Chi-Chi, black and white like her mother went to Lorna and her children in Inverness, along with Smudge's igloo where they were all born, just to ensure something of home would comfort her. Serendipity, the other tomcat, went to Himself's neice, Debbie who adored cats, and Sandy who said, 'You can't take that cat here. You know I don't like cats!' So I took him two cats. The Hobbit went with Serendipity, just to settle him in and give him confidence to deal with the farm dogs.

'When are you coming to take this cat of yours home?' Sandy implored, terrified he would be left with two hyper brothers, and of course, after a couple of weeks I took a rather reluctant Hobby back. He had had a ball! Soon I learned that Serendipity – they shortened it to Dippy – found a way to get his revenge on Sandy, who eventually grew very fond of the cat, despite this dastardly deed.

This of course, was all Smudge's fault.

If he left a shoe anywhere Dippy could access, the kitten peed in it. Poor man was caught out so often before he learned that shoes had to be left elsewhere rather than stop the otherwise clean cat. He never did it in Debbie's shoes, no more than Smudge ever did it in mine.

She was two years old before she had her kittens, and by then she had a serious fallout with Neil and found perfect retribution. She'd wait until he left a bag unattended as he prepared to travel out to work on the oil rigs, sneak in and do a little piddle in the middle of his pristine T-shirts! When the row erupted, she was never anywhere to be seen, and he had to leave before she sneaked back into the house. I was terrified she may take a dislike to a guest and get into a bedroom to do likewise. My heart would be in my mouth when I met her in a corridor, a place she frequently sneaked her way into, especially if guests left their bedroom door open. So bags were kept closed and rooms guarded against her. So, she just peed in Neil's shoes, no one else's. Just his. And Serendipity appeared to do the same, but only after he went to his new home, and never in Debbie's, only Sandy's.

'Neil, just don't leave footwear or bags around. It's not Smudge's fault,' I implored on behalf of the young cat who was one moment such a joy, next a nightmare. 'It's really Connie's fault.'

He looked at me aghast. No way did I ever blame Connie for anything. She was my right-hand, bringing into my busy life so much fun and laughter as well as taking a huge burden off my shoulders as she helped run The Sheiling for so many years.

First, I need to tell you how I ended up with a cat like Smudge after vowing, 'No more cats at The Sheiling.' We had Felix for 21 years and though she had her moments, we loved her to bits, she knew how to behave, treated the guests with great respect and allowed me to believe cats were easy-peasy in a busy guest house. But, when it became evident her years were coming to an end, the vet assured, she would know herself when to take her back to the surgery. She spent most of the next days in her special bed in the kitchen, not using a litter tray, barely moving. Was it time? Suddenly, she got out of her bed and ambled out the door to the toilet. She would not come back into the house again. She sat, staring up at me so intently. I knew it was time.

In the vet's I became so distressed when we were left for that short while to say goodbye to each other, I had to be let out a side door with my box. Felix was so poorly by then she didn't needed a basket to go to the vet, so they gave me a cardboard box to bring her back home. She is buried under a Caithness Flagstone in the centre of The Sheiling back green, surrounded by crocuses. I vowed I could never get another cat.

My first job was to write to so many of her friends, telling them that she would no longer be here to greet them when they arrived for their break that year. This was not an experience I wanted to repeat.

Life went on without a cat and Neil's then girlfriend Anne hinted we should have a dog. I closed my ears. But one fateful day, returning from Thurso with her, as we approached the local animal welfare centre she asked me to go in with her to see this dog. 'I'm not getting that dog, Anne,' I warned. She'd been going out with Neil for some time and stayed with us often when not at university and missed Felix, trying her best to persuade me to consider a rescue dog. I had enough on my hands and a barking dog would not enhance the welcome, or aid the peace I assured was part of our charm, of that I was convinced, so no dog.

The moment the car engine stopped I heard the loud persistent barking of this ex-guard dog she was convinced I could give a good home to!

'I just want to visit him then,' Anne assured, but as we were about to go to the kennels, a colleague of Anne's came in asking for a kitten. Like an idiot I agreed to go along with them all to view the only two kittens the home had.

As we waited in front of a long concrete indoor run, Mr Gunn went outside and shooed in a lovely little black cat, accompanied by a gorgeous jet black male kitten. Anne's friend bent down to stroke the cat and kitten but I could hear Mr Gunn stamping his feet and obviously trying to get the other kitten in through the hatch. Suddenly, in stormed a white ball of fur, with black splotches, prancing sideways on bandy front legs, arched back allowing for longer than normal back legs. The kitten stopped dead and stared at us. She then locked eyes on me and opened a remarkably pink mouth and hissed loudly. Green slanted eyes squinted in a white face with black mask covering eyes and ears. She had a jet black smudge on her nose, and black whiskers twitched against her white cheeks.

'Oh, look at Smudge,' I said. I should have known better. Within five minutes I was signing a cheque and Anne was cradling Smudge. We never did see the dog. And in the next five minutes this innocent looking creature had us breaking the speed limit with every window wide open as she proceeded to spray her displeasure all over the foot-well of the car, where Anne had quickly deposited her, our noses soon told us she had more than pee in her weaponry! We didn't know whether to laugh or cry. Tearing into the village, I spotted Connie attending cattle in a roadside field.

'Look what we have,' I shouted in triumph as if I had something to celebrate.

Reaching to stick her head in the open window, Connie drew back in horror, 'Oh, my god! What's that smell?' she gasped.

Braving the stink, she peered into the car where Smudge sat at Anne's feet, glaring up at us all. 'What possessed you?' she demanded, quickly stepping back.

'Well, it was that or a barking Alsatian,' I replied, holding my nose.

'How old is the Alsatian?'

'Twelve, and newly retired from the police force at Dounreay and not liking it one bit!' I retorted, anxious to get on our way up the road so the car, the cat, Anne and I too could rid ourselves of the evidence of Smudge's journey home.

But we weren't getting off that easy. 'Let me tell you then,' Connie said, nodding her head in deepening reassurances as she put her cards on the table and her nose to the wind. 'You would have given a good dog a good home for a good two years, and that would be good. You'll be stuck with that thing for the next 20 years!' It wasn't like her at all. She was a cat lover and it was from her home Felix came, so we thought we could rely upon her support in introducing a new cat to The Sheiling. Or rather, to Himself, who continued to work out in the North Sea.

Neil came in long after the cleaning up operation and thought the wee thing adorable. So far so good, and maybe we got Connie at a bad moment, up to her eyes with cattle.

'Well, what like?' she announced, coming in the back door next morning. I knew she meant the kitten, not me.

'Anne took her off to bed so I've not seen her yet.' The kitten had eaten a good supper and seemed to settle, though she merely sniffed at the litter tray we got for Felix's last few days with us when we thought her too ill to go out.

Arriving for breakfast with the kitten, Anne assured us she had been good as gold. I felt a surge of relief and laughed, 'Did she use the tray?'

The answer was cagey. 'No. She didn't have to.' I knew well there was something up.

'Did she poo all over you?' Connie chipped in, with a certain amount of hope. She sensed long before I did that this romance was reaching its final stages and already came down on the side of the boy she backed to the hilt, no matter what I said about him.

'Not me. She pooed all over Neil,' Anne announced in similar vein, then turned to me. 'Didn't you hear the shower running in the middle of the night? I'll take in the soiled linen after the house wash is done.' There was a smirk in her voice. Things were not too good then.

Connie wrinkled her nose in disgust. 'Should have taken the dog. Black and white cats are a force to be reckoned with!' Picking up the cleaning box she disappeared, humming to herself.

But with Anne back at university and Neil on the rig, it was Connie who cajoled the kitten into dealing with one of its many foibles: a terror of grass. 'Now, you listen here to me,' she quietly informed Smudge. 'Grass is not scary stuff, and you have to learn to walk on it because it's that – or a set of tacketty boots for you.'

Smudge had been used to a lot of concrete at the home in those days and had never set paw on grass. The minute you put her on grass, her back arched and she would lift one paw after the other to try and keep off it before dashing back to the safety of the concrete steps and pathways that surrounded the back door area. So Connie took to hoisting her onto the washing basket each time she made for the clothes rope and

Smudge had no option but to run over the grass to get to her beloved concrete.

What we never noticed was Smudge's pee on the damp washing as she sailed out in the basket towards the rope. With it drying for hours in the wind and sunshine before ironing, this was not noticed at first. Discovery meant no more sails in the washing basket! But for some time, a receptacle of any kind that held white cotton attracted her attention, especially if the cotton were damp. I listened to knowing pronouncements from Connie of, 'I told you so. Black and white cat. Trouble!' Eventually Smudge was persuaded out of the habit. Until Neil and Anne went their separate ways, and Anne went out of her life.

She missed Anne. I missed Anne too and at that time there was no other to keep an eye on Neil's comings and goings and Smudge took revenge by peeing on the T-shirts in Neil's bag, and eventually his shoes. She never did this to anyone else and had long ago stopped doing it on the linen. She never took actively against him. He had yet to commit the heinous crime that drew a spite you would not believe possible of a creature so devoted to those to whom she gave her favour. Nor could you believe it possible she could instil into her offspring, though only Serendipity, the propensity to pee in the shoes of those he saw fit to punish, as well as the few times he peed on Debbie's linen…but only when she had drawn his disapproval.

Chapter 7

*'I had been told that the training procedure with cats
is difficult. It's not. Mine had me trained in two days.'*

Bill Dana

Cat-astrophe!

The day after the introduction of Smudge to our lives,
Himself arrived home. The saucy little madam proceeded to
give him the biggest welcome out. She'd yet to utter a squeak,
and tiny though she was, she could use a trouser leg like
scaffolding and soon reached his face to stare into his eyes.
Her silence was the first characteristic that separated her from
other cats I had known. She never, ever mewed or purred, but
that stare could move mountains, and hearts. He fell for her
and they remained the firmest of friends throughout her long,
and difficult, life. Oh, she was happy. She was always happy,
but difficult.

She seemed to have her gastro bout under control, but
in her first few days, had yet to stand on anything outside other
than concrete, nor had she used the litter tray. She'd been
widdling on the linen, and had done all she had to do in Neil's
bed, with him in it, so she wasn't bothered. Himself and I had
to go out together, such a rare thing in itself, me finding less
and less time to socialise, coinciding with Himself's
diminishing inclination, so it had to be one of the many
funerals we rushed off to. You could decline a wedding or
party invitation, but missing a funeral was seriously frowned
upon.

'Isn't it wonderful to be going out together,' we
invariably said, eyeing each other's sombre garb as we headed
for various grave yards. We hadn't quite reached the age when

friends and relatives began to pop off at a regular rate, but in rural communities, it is expected to attend most funerals as a mark of respect, no matter your opinion of the poor soul awaiting burial, there being no local crematorium and the thought of burning the body being alien to most people's beliefs, at that time.

That afternoon we returned and the stench hit us as we came in the door. Smudge was nowhere to be seen. Visitors were arriving the next day and the house was spick and span. The doors to all rooms remained open. Still, the hall fire door accessing the bedroom corridor was closed so where was the pong coming from.

I nosed my way all around the front lounge, the dining room, then tackled the shower room, the kitchen, my office. Nothing. But the smell got stronger as we made our way upstairs. In our bedroom a little nose poked from under the bed.

I stroked her silky coat. 'It's not your fault, pet, but where did you do it.'

A long search eventually led us to a waste-paper bin, in the twin room opposite, with the liner very nearly folded over the doings. I began to worry, not that she wouldn't use the tray and chose a bin, but that the tummy problem had not gone away.

Next morning, first thing, in to the vet. I put the litter bin and Felix's igloo in the back of the car, but by now Smudge looked pathetic, so I wrapped her up in a towel and placed her on my knee where she lay, staring intently up into my face.

'You'll have to leave her in. She's very dehydrated and needs to be put on a drip.'

We spent an anxious day, none more so than Connie who never called her anything but the black and white cat behind her back, when she got up to no good, and Smudgie to her face as they proceeded to bond and make friends with each other. After a couple of days we were told her tummy was settled and we could take her home.

I took the towel in with me, scrunched up on the passenger seat and there she elected to sit. She seemed bright as a button, in no time reaching up with her paws to the window. I was driving fairly slowly, hoping there would be no road checks between Thurso and Melvich when a car drew up behind that I assumed would overtake when safe. Smudge shot into the back seat and up on to the rear window shelf. There were children in the car. I could see their faces in the mirror as their car closed in on mine. She was prancing about the back parcel shelf and had their full attention. No way were they going to overtake until we reached their turn off.

She lost interest in the back perch and came in to sit on the towel, happy as a wee sand boy. 'Were you pulling faces at the children?' Nothing would have surprised me. I always talk to the animals I travel with, and no, I don't expect any answers and having travelled with some pretty vociferous ones, Smudge was by far the quietest, but the one who always got her point across. Connie welcomed her with open arms and the day proceeded.

I was there to greet the guests and showing them into the front double, we were amicably going through the welcome routine when the woman screamed. My heart stopped.

Turning round to look at her stricken face, as she stared at the double bed, I saw it for myself. The padded bedcover had moved. You just do not expect that when viewing your room. It was a heavy lined cover, made to measure, fitted with a pleated valance. Did we imagine that movement? It now looked perfectly still. No way could you say there was something there until a low slither to the side, followed by a plop on to the floor and Smudge popped out. She slowly sashayed out of the room, leaving our precious guests on their first time visit…wondering.

I was so embarrassed. Were we a 5-Star establishment 18 years ago when this happened? If not, we had to be 4-Star, and no way should a cat, even though a little kitten, have been in the room, never mind between the bedcover and the duvet. I offered to change the covers, but they laughed, no allergies, so no problem. For them, so long as we kept her out of their room, there was no problem but for us, the gastro problems were back so little wonder my anxiety levels soared the minute I saw Smudge tear into the guest area.

'She's a little cutie,' the man said. It was always the men who fell for Smudge.

Passing, Connie viewed the crime scene and announced, 'Black and white cat! Told you so!' It became one of her party pieces whenever it could be enacted, and you'd be surprised how often Smudge gave cause. But that didn't close us down, nor was it the gastro problem.

Back in the kitchen, Connie assured the kitten, 'There you go, Smudgie. That's your toilet all sorted.' Persevering with the tray was futile. 'You're as well to give in. A black and white cat always wins, Joan. I told you!' So it was the plastic waste-paper bin, with the requisite lining. The bedroom now sported a new bin and despite several attempts to put cat litter into Smudge's bin, it had to be a bin liner. We would hear it rustle on the occasions she headed for the back lobby to use her bin. She never failed to neatly parcel it up, fully expecting a fresh bin liner for the next time.

Again we headed for the vet's at Thurso. After another stay we were told she was fine. 'I can't understand it. She's no sooner home than she's got tummy problems again. 'Well, I hope you don't have to bring her back,' one of the busy vets said. 'She certainly knows how to make a nuisance of herself.'

I had never in my life heard any of the vets complain about an animal. She looked so small and sweet, wrapped in her towel, ready for the journey home. 'What does she do?'

What could she do, tucked into their pens with a drip in her paw. 'Was she trying to pull out the drip?'

'Oh, no. She was very good about that. But every time one of us passed her pen, her paw shot out like a grappling hook and grabbed our coats. And these claws are razor sharp. I was tempted to snip them.'

'Oh, you can't do that. She's just a little moggy and she's going to be a hunting cat.' All our cats were hunters. It was my excuse for having them. They needed their claws.

'You hope!' But that was the last visit to the vet over that problem.

We had her now for over a week and the next two days she had no tummy problems. We kept the doors pinned open to access the dining room, guest lounge and bedrooms while we worked in the mornings. The first time she went completely missing, we combed the house and the garage. The path to the garage passed through the patio so this was safe, no grass to scare her, therefore the garage became part of her new territory. But she wasn't there. Eventually, a tiny movement from the vegetable basket drew us to her hiding place. It was three tiered on wheels and well packed. She was snuggled down between the leaves of a cabbage and some broccoli.

'Dump them, Connie. I'm shopping this afternoon and I'll get back early with more for dinner.' We were doing our best to keep the kitten away from everything, and sleeping in among the fresh veg meant I couldn't use them. 'Damn it, Connie, I never thought she's kip in there.'

'Black and white cat. Trouble. I warned you.'

'Connie. What black and white cat did you have that caused nothing but trouble?'

'We never had one…ever. They're trouble, so we never kept a black and white kitten. What about you and the cats you've had? Did you never come across a black and white one?'

'Yes, my father's cat was black and white.'

'She would have been a nice, quiet, amenable creature then?' The sarcasm dripped.

'Well, not exactly,' I had to admit, 'Hey, we had one for a while. She was black and white.'

'Yes, and she was trouble.'

Pat's daughter, Hazel, had taken Felix's kitten, Samantha, but was so stressed out with her tearing up curtains and fighting with their dogs that she gave the young cat to her sister-in-law. She was much loved there until the new baby arrived. Samantha opted to sleep in the baby's pram, so Samantha was seeking a new home again. I took her back and Felix was furious. She made poor Sammy's life a misery. One day my friend Shirley called when Sammy was sitting out of Felix's way, on the ironing board, looking beautiful.

'Did you know Corina's cat just died and she is so upset.' This was the daughter of my friend, Barbara Jappy, who eventually built a house much closer to us and became a valued helper at The Sheiling. Samantha went to live with them in their original home. This cat's closest friend was my horse, Bronco, and I still have an old photo taken of Sammy riding the horse. She was lucky. Corina had a pony and the cat, after all her troubles went to a fantastic home where she ruled the roost. They had lived semi-detached to Joey's home and when Sammy's family were out, she jumped on to Joey's window sill and rubbed her paw up and down the glass until the squeaking got one of them to come to the door. She wouldn't go in, but raced round to her own door where they retrieved the key and let her in to her own house. No fool, this black and white cat!

'Sammy was just clever, Connie, not trouble, and so was my father's cat.'

'Trouble, Joan, and you should have known better,' was her last word on the subject and I began to wonder. As I got on with sorting out the breakfasts, my mind drifted back to

69

the cats at Kirtomy, trying to remember any as difficult as this new kitten.

One particular day when the cats made their way back from a hidey-hole at the rear of the old tumble-down pig-sty behind our home in Kirtomy, three beautiful slate-grey kittens were shepherded between them. This was not a colour we had ever seen on a kitten before. And, of course, the kittens were tame. I knew where they were while others followed the suspect mother pleading, 'Where have you got that kittens?' her new slim shape giving her away. This time the cats had outfoxed their arbiters.

I waited in fear of what would happen to them. But our mother was resourceful as well as kind and found homes in the village. Having achieved this miracle, I would not have dared baulk at delivering each to its new abode. As they grew, I treasured each moment spent with them, never before having three kittens to keep me entranced, grudgingly getting into the car that took the Kirtomy children the four mile journey to school in Bettyhill each day, caring nothing for lessons, only about getting back to the cats.

Eventually I was persuaded to put all three into a basket and make the long, sad, walk to the Overside with my precious cargo, such a coincidence that the three identical kittens should go to the three Dollys who lived there. Being used to me carting them about since birth, they made no attempt to escape. One went to Dolly Campbell, her home being quite far away and having no young children, we were not familiar with that fireside; the other to Dolly Mackay, a home frequently visited as Dolly was dearly loved by us all, her door permanently open and her grandchild, Doris, a close friend of Muriel's. We were much more wary of the man of the house, Jimmy or Seamus, the Gaelic sobriquet, which better suited him, to which was added the epithet Duke, to distinguish him from Hamish's grandfather, Seamus Ruadh, or so we were told when we asked our inevitable 'Whys?' But that was stretching the truth as most were nicknames and many derisory.

Unlike today's children, gossip was debated well away from our ears. And to ensure our ignorance, the village had a cunning plan. They lapsed into Gaelic and made sure we understood as little of it as they felt was good for us, thus endangering an ancient language! How clever was that, pointing the finger at us, being the first generation to lose Gaelic. Our parents' excuse being the difficulties they had when going out into the world or attending school for the first time as a native Gaelic speaker. A crash course in English saw many an unpleasant punishment in days when the tawse was liberally administered in place of patience and understanding.

Seamus was the proud owner of Ben, the black and white cat's antagonist, and despite the dog's uncertain temper, there were cows and sheep to work, his skills held in high esteem, hence the lecture we got on the outrageous behaviour of our cat. 'She could have taken an eye out of him,' was the response to our defensive cries, 'She's far smaller than Ben,' followed by, 'He started it, anyway!' We never split on our father by telling Seamus that Dad was inordinately proud of his cat who got an extra titbit that night for defending Kirtomy Mains so well, or that Merran never shouted at the black and white cat to get off her land.

Kirtomy Mains was the address given to all the houses on the west side of the village burn, derived from the one original house and farm, built after the great clearances of people from good inland pastures to make way for sheep. From this cruel policy came the coastal villages that sprung up along the coastline; a long and sad history of how the poor were exploited by their landlords, under the guise of moving them for their own good. Just like rubbing the cat's nose in it for its own good. Bet the cat never saw it as such any more than the people who scraped a living from the meagre earth clinging to the rocky shoreline. They fished their dead out of a sea they knew nothing of, except that in learning to respect its moods, they could possibly enhance their diet and hope to survive. And that is why we have the seaboard crofting communities we live in today, augmented less and less by the fruits of the sea, or the produce of the land, as the financial necessities of today's lifestyles far outweigh what once kept families alive, and together, those who did not become the diaspora of the Commonwealth countries when evicted from their inland pastures. Yet we still listen to the plaintiveness of a Gaelic lament, paying homage to a time when animals were more important than people, otherwise, an episode of our history then laid to rest in our educational years, until now, when culture studies allows a look back into a murky past.

Behind that first house in the village of Kirtomy was a walled-in communal garden. All who lived on that west side of the burn were entitled to a plot where carrots and cabbages were the main fare as tatties were planted in the fields, and swedes were grown by the crofters for their sheep, in huge numbers, given out to those in favour and greatly appreciated. What fun on a moonlit night to sneak into a field of swedes and help yourself, but no way could you take your spoils home; that was stealing, so we ate them like apples, there being no opportunity to do a bit of scrumping in Kirtomy's treeless grounds.

But to get back to those days when each villager knew every other inhabitant well, the children as familiar as their elders with the entire neighbourhood, the last of our three slate-grey kittens went to Dolly MacIvor. Being a house with children, these kittens would be sure to be seen again, but once gone from our home, they were gone from our lives. Cats were always busy creatures, seeing to their appetites, so we saw little of other people's felines. However, my mother met Doris making her way along the road, pushing her little pram with the hood up against the wind. She had a favourite teddy bear called Tangles, trundled everywhere, dolled up in baby clothes.

My mother pulled down the buttoned up rain cover, as you would to admire a new baby, ready with a warm comment on Tangles' welfare. 'And how is Tangles today, Doris?' she politely enquired, peering under the hood.

'My goodness!' Her head sprang back as she looked into the staring, slanted, green eyes of a fully grown, very large, fluffy marmalade cat, lying flat on its back, paws relaxed over the top covers, decked out in mittens, a matinee jacket and a woolly hat with satin bow tied firmly under the cat's chin. This docile creature was so used to being dressed up and carted about, it just lay there and thought of fish. That very same cat had me dash out of Doris's home, crying in terror when I walked in the open door and there was Seamus, in his usual chair by the fire. He had the cat held between his knees, wrapped in a jute bag, with only its head sticking out.

I looked on anxiously…until he reached into his back pocket, took out his tobacco knife and flicked it open. I screamed and took off. It was later explained to me that the cat was not about to have its throat cut, but a fish bone – Seamus was one of the few small boat fishermen in Kirtomy at that time – had stuck in the cat's mouth, and Seamus, who was very fond of the cat, was about to release it from its misery by removing the fishbone without getting scratched in the process.

I never dressed up my cats or treated them in any way other than as a cat, but in time we had another dog to go along with Brandy. It was an affable Cairn Terrier called Fraochie, Gaelic for heather, and Muriel spent much of her time dressing up the dog in old baby clothes.

'Lassie, is that the dog you have there?' our father asked, peering into the depth of a shawl as she rocked the dog gently in her arms. Nothing more would be said because if the dog didn't like it, the dog would not be lying there.

Other memories flood back, like the morning our mother summoned me through to the bedroom known as the Far-off room where an end window gave a good view of the road. 'Come and see this, Joan,' she called. I knew by her tone of voice it was safe to go. Sandra and I shared the bedroom and our mother despaired when finding heaps of our clothes turfed over the back of the basket chair rather than hung up in the wardrobe, but this time her voice sounded animated. Certain calls sped me off in the opposite direction as far as my long legs would carry me. And by golly, I had occasion to know who I took my turn of speed from. I once got caught sneaking a look at a cake in the new gas oven, an intriguing contraption, a far cry from the oven at the side of the big black range in the kitchen, where my mother would angrily shoo out a cat who sought comfort in the warming drawer underneath the oven, someone having left the door open.

I must have been a feisty child as my earliest memory of my father was of this strange man, tearing down the partition between the scullery with its water cupboard, working table and food cupboards, and the closet, a cosy bedroom with room for little else but the bed and the washstand that held the trappings of the night's needs. I stared at this unknown man who was wrecking our home. 'Go home to your own house and break it down!' I howled and began to attack him with outraged gusto. To be told this was my father meant little as I didn't really know what a father was, born as I was three years before the war ended. I vaguely remember a Granny Kirtomy, but she had vanished by then, and I knew little of a man who was rarely home during the war. Now the war was over, his first job was to enlarge the scullery and make it more useful as a working kitchen, but it was a long time after that before what we knew as the kitchen became known as the living room! However, the scullery was always known as the scullery even when water was piped into the house and a sink was placed under the window, a fridge installed and the old water cupboards turned into modern worktops.

Not long after removing the scullery wall, a new-fangled gas cooker was installed, my mother's pride and joy, despite the encumbrance of the attached gas cylinder. Soon, enticing smells wafted from this new accessory. And, of course, I had to investigate. 'Close that door at once,' my mother shouted, horror struck, rationing still making ingredients scarce. I obeyed, with such a bang, she feared her precious cake would collapse. She yelled in horror. I was past her in a flash and tore down the garden path heading for Merran's Brae with an irate parent racing after me. Such was her anger she reached half-way down the brae before giving it up as a lost cause, me dashing towards sanctuary on the Overside, shocked my mother could run so fast, and that she would actually run so far. Like so many other things, by the time hunger drove me home it was all forgotten.

The day she called me into the Far-Off room, she pointed out the window and there was the black and white cat, walking down the road, tail held high, behind her the one small kitten allowed from the latest litter. Taking up the rear, assiduously looking to right and left came Fluffy, their catch of the day firmly gripped between her teeth. They were coming from the fields and teaching their young charge how to hunt. The kitten was soon to be homed, but we had Fluffy and the black and white cat long after I left at the age of 12 for what was popularly known as further education.

After the war, postal addresses were changed to include the sorting office various villages came under, so wc had to include Thurso, Caithness, in our address despite Kirtomy being located in Sutherland. I thought this heinous as the huge map that almost filled one wall of our primary class-room in Bettyhill, separated out the counties of Scotland in interesting colours. If you ignored the Shetland and Orkney Islands, allocated to their box in the top right hand corner of the map, first of the mainland counties was Caithness, and coloured a sickly yellow, with Ross-shire on the south side of Sutherland a shade of salmon pink that did not impress me, but Sutherland was clad in a beautiful milky green that filled me with superiority. I lived in the best coloured, and certainly the largest, county on the map. Belonging to Sutherland was always a source of pride. Yet, on the two occasions in my life I was lauded for achieving something special, the media had me well and truly a Cathnessian, and nothing I could do about it! Everywhere I go, I'm told I come from Caithness because of that postal address.

When Shank's pony was the only option, my mother would take those of her brood capable of the walk – more importantly, capable of behaving themselves for a day – and set off on the mile long hike to the Pole, a stone pillar box for posting letters, standing at the junction of the Kirtomy road end and the main coastal road, now dubbed the Scenic Tourist Route to impress visitors to this area. There isn't another route, not if you want to get to the seaboard communities along that main A836 towards the West, or moving East, until you pass the Split Stone and into the rich agricultural lands of Caithness, leaving behind the outstandingly beautiful, crofting lands of Sutherland with its backdrop of mountains, the land fringed in silver sands and rocky shores.

Each time I was part of the entourage heading for Thurso, along would come our cat. I used to wail in abject misery, pleading to wait with the cat for fear it would get lost or killed long before we could get back. I was usually dragged aboard the bus to go visit friends or into the small county town for a precious day's shopping, an empty suitcase the usual means of transporting the wares back home. I remember once visiting my mother's friend who eventually came to live in Kirtomy but was first housed, and cosily too, in a black Nissen hut close to the runway at the old aerodrome at Dounreay, long before it became an Atomic Power Station. The bus did not arrive back at the Pole for the length of a day I spent in happy compliance, forgetting about the cat as this treat was too precious to spend fretting.

There, waiting for us upon our return, always hiding way up on top of a rocky, heather-clad outcrop on the opposite side of the road, out bounded our cat with gleeful meows. Any growing anxiety as the mail bus meandered through its many stops were turned into leaps of joy as I skipped happily home, cat racing in front, she as pleased as I to see all was well.

Fluffy in particular, had an unerring instinct of knowing which bedroom I slept in, calling to me in the night, and of course, I would get up and let her in, cosy her down under the blankets until I let her out again in the morning. If found out, trouble followed. As a teenager I took painful quinsy throats and on one occasion became so ill the doctor was called, a rare occasion in our household. He threw back the bedclothes to examine me and out popped a cat.

'I was never so black affronted in all my life,' our mother scolded for days to come. She was proud of the esteem she was held in by our local practitioner, Dr MacRae, whose advice to a villager may well be, 'Go and see Marion. She'll have what you're needing.' Imagine that happening nowadays. There would be an outcry! There was only one communal telephone, accessed in the lobby of the local postman, the only Post Office being miles away in Bettyhill. The doctor also lived miles away, in Armadale and was happy to dish out advice over the phone, unless the need was urgent, hence the services of my mother would be called although she never in her life did a nursing course. Instead, she nursed our father's aging parents, each eventually bedridden about the same time as she sent her oldest daughter to the Kirtomy school, ran after a three year old and brought our younger brother into the world. And all without the aid of indoor water or electricity.

Her common sense and propensity to keep a medicine cabinet as well-stocked as her larder gave her a leading edge in addressing a problem before it got out of hand. However, her best asset was her ability to keep her mouth shut when it came to other people's business. We all grew up with a horror of

77

calling in a doctor unless there was no other option, respecting as did so many in this vast area that one single doctor covered, that he went days and nights, snatching sleep when he could. He had, of course, the district nurses to rely upon and they were worth their weight in gold. One was Dolly and Sheamus' daughter Dorothy, but at the time I write of, she was doing her training, though later years brought her back to the district to become one of the most respected nurses ever to work with the people. She became known as Dorothy-the-Nurse, and is still recognised by that name today!

During one of the worst storms of my youth, though not the night many community halls were damaged by the ferocity of the storm and the Bettyhill hall was completely blown away, our mother ensured we were all safe as the howling wind and rattling rain battered against the window panes. The only reason she removed me to sanctuary in her own bedroom was the fear I would open a window to let in the cat. One of her bedroom windows faced out over the North sea where the gale blew in from. She was not a woman given to fanciful fears but I have a strong memory of lying beside her in bed facing that northerly window as she shielded our faces with a blanket held in front of us, fearful the strength of the storm would blow in the window. Above the howls of the wind and the lash of the rain, all I could hear were the wails of my favourite cat, our first Fluffy, having jumped up on the henhouse and then leapt on to the windowsill, begging for sanctuary from the storm. I plagued and I pestered and at last she went down and opened the east facing door, but to no avail as the cat had no idea, wanting only that I should let her in the window as usual. Whatever room I slept in, the cat could find me.

In the morning with the storm abated, there the cat was, unharmed, washing her face on the kitchen windowsill, waiting to get in. There are many more memories of the cats in our lives, good memories, and a few bad, better forgotten, but I do not know of a single day that we did not have a cat.

And I had to go and marry a dog man.

Chapter 8

'Heaven goes by favour. If it goes by merit, you would stay out and your dog would go in.'

Mark Twain

Every Dog Has Its Day

Early this Friday morning, the last day in August 2012, listening to the news as I debated on when exactly I would persuade Himself out of bed to face the day, I heard the word feral in reference to two different species. One of course was cats.

In the middle of agreeing that OK, if pressed, I would reverse normal and get up first, the radio announced that the Scottish Wild Cat survey recently carried out proved there are fewer than 250 breeding pairs left in Scotland and that the strain is being diluted through breeding with domestic cats gone feral. However, the project to neuter feral cats would continue.

'See,' I said to my spouse's retreating back, luxuriating into the extra space as I continued to lie in bed. 'I hit this neutering stuff at the right time. It's to save the wild cats. You'd approve of that.' I felt justified as he was still a bit apprehensive about me taking on more work, and to him Cats Protection spelled work.

'Aye, but I sometimes wonder if you do all this gadding about just to save you staying at home like a normal person.' Never did I leave home on any business without ensuring the tins were full of baking and the freezer held meals for the duration. But he stemmed any response by putting on the shower full pelt. He was good at getting his point across and ensuring my reply went unheard. And good too at wielding the dishcloth, and washing up, and playing a bossy second fiddle to my preparations for buffets and dinner parties, but he does not allow himself learn the rudiments of cooking. As for shopping, that was scary stuff, a step too far for that old dog he professed himself to be when he retired from the oil rigs and decided he would take over the running of The Sheiling, without as much as a by your leave cast in my direction. I wouldn't go so far as to say there was blood on the carpet, but the ensuing years in the business, as told in *Heads On Pillows* and *Bye Bye B&B*, had their moments!

The 'Old dogs don't learn new tricks,' mantra was worn thin as we came to a dubious agreement on who would do what, and when. But when the old dog realised new tricks paid for his supper, the old dog soon played ball – except for cooking and shopping, and of course making beds, and sorry, ironing was quite out of the question. He was no chauvinist, but there were limits to his willingness to mix and match the work rota. Especially when his better half disappeared for a day furthering the cause of tourism that took from his coffers rather than added to them! And now he no longer had a public to serve, and plenty of outdoor work to keep him happy, he was wary I may get carried away and not cope with what I took on in moments of magnanimity that crept upon me every now and again.

By now my attention was taken up by a news item about the amount of young children who murdered, raped, robbed and generally caused mayhem by running feral. I thought we ran wild in our early days, free to roam the perimeters of the village, but feral? That is a different concept. As children we heard little of what went on in the outside world and then, at the tip of their tongues our parents had the means to keep everything from us: their use of the Gaelic language. In the early days of growing up in Kirtomy, the village was steeped in Gaelic but there appeared to be a consensus of opinion that English was the spoken language in front of the children.

This was an ill-informed decision and by the time my son's generation came along, Gaelic was a dirty word. Yet today my grandson opted for Gaelic rather than French for his second language studies due to the revival of the language and the funds ploughed into its resurrection. Those talented Gaelic musicians and media-smart broadcasters make Gaelic cool! However, ensuring we grew up fluent in English had a great advantage that had little to do with education. It allowed the older generation to gossip indiscriminately with child at foot.

Nevertheless, with the majority of homes having grandparents who were more comfortable speaking their native tongue, Gaelic was picked up by the older children. With the onset of World War II taking most of the men away, and grandparents going to their eternal rest, this left mothers to continue their children's preparation for school by using only English in their presence.

That's what happened in our household, allowing Sandra a fair grip of the tongue used to hold forth on matters beyond our understanding, or so we led them to believe.

'Does she speak Gaelic,' someone asked with a juicy morsel to impart.

'No,' my mother answered in Gaelic, followed by 'But you won't sell her,' meaning, watch what you say, she'll pick up some of it.

I, like most of the children, knew swear words, weather predictions, greetings, utterings of general disgust, and most innocuous proclamations, but following a conversation was totally beyond me. Words like *plàighich* had no need of translation. If I wanted to know anything of the current scandal that rocked the village, I had to believe what Sandra told me. Needless to say, there were activities I had a very colourful take on.

One of our ploys came about when we knew our mother was preparing food in the scullery for an evening of entertaining neighbours. Many evenings saw at least one neighbour arriving for an hour or two, there being no TV to destroy the great art of conviviality sprinkled with much laughter, and no doubt lots of gossip, but when the company was mixed with the children in attendance, stories of old came out to fascinate and enthral and were repeated in English, with liberal sprinklings of Gaelic to camouflage the naughty bits! When only the women got together, Sandra and I would sneak into the kitchen, settle ourselves under the square table in front of the east facing recessed window, the long chenille table-cloth and generous curtains covering our deception. It was usually a cat's curiosity that gave us away, but we gleaned a few tit-bits before being flushed out and shooed up the stairs, with the warning ringing in our ears, 'You'll answer for this in the morning!' We never did! My mother's bark was well and away far scarier than her bite.

Given no tuition whatsoever from our parents on the birds and the bees, I thought sex was for the Gaelic language only. And no way was a teacher going to fill in any gaps in our biological progression. Any mention of bodily bits said in the heat of battle was severely punished. We had no bike-shed either to gain knowledge behind, no doubt making the learning curve all the more unfathomable when we shared our gleanings with each other, skulking in the lee of a dyke. Under such a blanket of secrecy tis little wonder so many children grew up to believe their grannies were their mothers, the patter of tiny feet not the planned outcome, like today when young girls are keen to start a family to get on the housing ladder and be assured of government support. Support usually came from grannies accepting the role of mother to the additional child, with none daring to furnish us children with the truth of the matter.

There was government assistance of a kind in those early days too, doled out by the person we knew as The Kind

Man. We children thought him incredibly rich because he had one of the few cars we saw and despite the language barrier we learned he gave out largesse to certain people only, comments made in hushed tones behind cupped hands as curtains twitched in a bid to see where The Kind Man was going today.

Pocket money was unheard of but I must have had the entrepreneurial spirit somewhere in my genes as I had my own method of adding to the precious half-crowns doled out by parents and grannies on birthdays. I scoured the dumps on our side of the village for empty jam jars and lemonade bottles with their intriguing screw tops, cleaned at the wells built into the land behind the houses. God help you if you were caught taking the wooden lid off the well and possibly contaminating the fresh sweet drinking water hauled home daily in white enamel pails.

One memorable day Hamish and his older sister Mary set off with Sandra and me to scour the dumps. They held a fascination of objects: purple bottles, ribbed and corked, sometimes contents trickling out when emptied; old broken chamber pots, rose covered, known as chanties and no doubt mourned now they were no longer fit for purpose; the odd screw topped beer bottle; a broken piggan, that stone hot-water bottle that held its heat until the morning throughout the coldest of nights. But this day we found a high-heeled shoe, delicate long pointed toe, fine leather with buttoned strap across the instep, and well past its best. The other shoe was nowhere to be seen.

This find greatly impressed us. We took our shoe to a house closest to the dump where we suspected it came from. A very old sister and brother lived in its dark interior. In our sneaking under the table opportunities, we gleaned the story that in his younger days, the brother Dunny had spent 12 years in the box bed in the kitchen with precious little wrong with him until the decision – no doubt lacking in medical consultation – was reached that a fire set under the bed may get

84

him out! Our translation from the Gaelic just could have been suspect, but it added to our awe of the residents! The sister kept herself to herself, so it was a house we were warned not to include in our wanderings. Taken there once by my mother, I saw the box bed, and the scary old people, draped in soulful black. No way was I ever going back there. The old woman, Aine, intrigued me with her long black clothes and gnarled appearance. But that did not stop me being party to any opportunity to tease, that being part of our growing need to find entertaining pass times.

We set this intriguingly different, and ever so posh, dilapidated shoe on top of an old fence post standing sentinel long after the fence disappeared giving the post a prominent position right in front of Dunny's house. Then we danced round the post, shouting at the top of our voices, 'Aine Ross's dancing shoe, Aine Ross's dancing shoe!' on and on until at last the door flew open and Dunny appeared. Without further ado, he fired an old blunderbuss over our heads. We took off like hares, howling with fright, then collapsing with laughter in an old crowe, one of the old original stone-built houses, the rafters long gone, and the earth floors soft with the lush growth of a century of neglect. Did we tell Dunny had shot at us? We may have been wicked but we weren't stupid. Our mothers would have killed us for our lack of respect and blackening their good names, always a heinous crime.

Now and again, Hamish and I would spend hours at the Kirtomy Burn, watching trout swim upstream, selecting one special fish, skilfully enticing it into a prepared side pool where a tickle under its tummy guided it into our waiting pail. We hurried our catch to Jimmy Oag, who was a keen cleaner of the shared well. We put the trout in the well, assured by Jimmy that the trout kept the well clean.

Patting Tworky's head, he warned, 'Now, you be sure to come back here in two days. Two days, after school, no sooner. And no later than that. Then take your trout back to the burn. You must be very careful not to hurt him and then he'll tell his pals what a lovely holiday he had in the well.' We loved the trout in the burn and tales of Tammy Troot on Children's Hour encouraged our belief they could clean the well. We would never dream of putting a vile hook into their mouths and we believed everything Jimmy Oag told us.

'How does he clean the well, Jimmy?' we asked.

'He has a wee scrubbing brush, stored at the back of the well.'

We peered into a depth that reached back to the source of fresh spring water. The floor glistened, made up of stones rounded by the pounding of the sea and carted from the shore by Jimmy himself, and Tworky, of course. We knelt on the Caithness flagstone that fronted this precious commodity, where the water pail sat as you filled it, lugging it home, two hands gripping the wooden grip on the wire handle, spilling most of the precious contents. We loved catching the trout and would do anything that pleased Jimmy Oag. Our well cleaning operations came to a halt when my mother discovered we'd been doing this for years.

She threw up her hands in horror. 'You're about to turn my stomach.' Her stomach was easily turned, especially when Sandra and I constantly hauled home tadpoles and newts, keeping them in massive glass jars in the shed, until we had to stop because we were about to turn her stomach.

Liptons and the Co-op were our mobile grocery vans and my excitement knew no bounds as I trudged my occasional haul of bottles and jars to their counters, vying with Hamie Lad over ownership of such bounty. Our many bargaining chips allowed us share the loot with a steely eye kept on any agreement.

I would have been about eight when Merran made the unbelievable announcement she was going off to visit family in Canada. Anyone leaving the village for distant shores was worthy of much critique. But Merran? Surely not.

Before she departed on this momentous adventure she placed a tin box of her most treasured papers, and her dog, into the custody and care of our mother. That trip to Canada caused me one of the biggest hidings of my life. It was at a time when you couldn't take any clothes out of the country, or maybe into another country, whichever, without first washing them, and at a time when I was well advised, I should have been old enough to know better. Her trip to foreign shores caused some speculation amongst the wits in the village, and one fine day, with a fresh wind blowing off the land, Hamish and I discovered Merran's washing line as we'd never seen it before, bloomers, stockings, vests and such like unmentionables billowing in the breeze.

We howled with laughter, pointing out each item of personal adornment. We whooped and hollered and danced around this feast for the eyes, knowing we had sight of what others merely speculated on. We had Swannie with us and she joined in the fun, leaping and dancing, making grabs at the clothes, adding to our glee. Until a screech came from behind the house.

'Swannie! Come away at once! And just you wait till I see your mothers.'

Our mothers soon laid into us with tongue and hand and only the knowledge of such retribution restored Merran's dignity. What punishment was doled out to Swannie we never knew but, the dog being part of our play, we knew our canine friend was not allowed over the door at certain times anyway. We put this down to Merran's curmudgeonly nature, never being told it was to ensure Swannie remained a virgin. She was called after her owner's heroine, the author Annie S. Swan, whose books lined Merran's dresser where many would have plates. Swannie had a reputation to keep up.

After Merran's send off, Swannie slept in our barn with freedom never known to her. Such was her diet, she soon put on weight. We thought nothing of it. Not until that inevitable day when our mother arrived back from bringing the dog's breakfast down to her just before the school car picked us up to take us to Bettyhill. It took a lot to shake our mother, but she was in an obvious state of high distress. We thought the weight the dog put on was due to the high living she partook of, never believing there could be any other reason.

'What is that woman going to say?' our mother bemoaned as I flew down to the barn to discover the cause of anything that could turn this strong woman into a quivering wreck.

I could not believe my eyes.

There, snug beside a dog that had kept her secret better than most adults, lay one fat, squirming, black puppy, nothing like his mother. So many working dogs had that colouring, it was impossible to say which had done the dirty deed. Ben may have braved the black and white cat. Or Swannie may have been adventurous, making her way to the Overside when our mother's back was turned and we were at school, but the finger of accusation pointed at Ben. It definitely wasn't Tworky. He was far too innocent, brought up on baby talk and kept always at his master's side. It didn't matter. My whole life changed. I thought it was a true miracle – my mother thought it an unmitigated disaster.

I fell completely in love, forgot all about cats, and named the puppy Rex before it opened its unfocused dark eyes to look into my totally focused blue-grey ones. I had one target in mind. I never shut up, I just niggled on, and on, and on.

'You cannot keep that puppy,' was the constant response to my constant pleadings. It was long before Brandy's time, Neil not much more than a toddler.

'Do you, yourself, think Merran would let you have Swannie's puppy after what you did to her?'

'I wouldn't do that if I had my own dog.' I made all sorts of promises and bargains. Merran would soon be home. My mother dreaded her arrival as much as I did.

'What if she drowns Rex?' was my best threat, the little creature by now having his own character as Merran's stay in Canada was by no means a short holiday. Even then I knew that once you named an animal, you had a bond, and I knew our parents would never allow drowning to happen. It was my best bargaining tool.

Eventually I got an answer I could deal with. 'You'll have to ask your father,' came when my exasperated mother was worn down with constant lobbying.

'Dad, what are you going to do with Swannie's puppy? Are you going to drown Rex?' His face looked stricken. He may have been a hard man as he saw to the safety of his crew, fighting the vagaries of the sea, yet ensuring his fishing trips were lucrative enough when seas were rough, to guarantee the crew had a very good living. His boat did not achieve the accolade of Scotland's top seine netter for nothing. At home he was a pussy-cat! It was our mother who was the lioness, ever watchful, ever ready to protect, or cuff, her cubs, but always fair in her dealings.

'Lassie! We don't drown puppies.'

'Swannie says I can have her puppy. Mam says I have to ask you?'

'Me? Does your mother say you can have it?'

'Mam says I can keep Rex if you say it's OK.'

'Oh, well, if that's what she says then,' and all thoughts of drowning puppies expunged from his thoughts, he went back to reading the Fishing News. I took that as a yes and was over the moon, but I had a lot to learn. Merran's holiday must have mellowed her nature as she seemed quite taken with the puppy and delighted it had a good home. Rex became my shadow. I have a strong memory of suffering my first real bout of homesickness that first year I left him behind to go on holiday.

Sandra and I spent as long of our summer holidays as we could in Scullomie, the birth place of our mother, where

Granny Scullomie was treated as a queen by her daughter-in-law Dinah, and her son Sandy. Their three sons, and the indisputable attraction of a working croft populated with many animals lured us there, year on year.

That year, not long after I arrived, now old enough to go to Scullomie on my own, travelling on the Mail bus and walking the mile from the road end to where I knew I would be warmly welcomed, it wasn't long before I began to feel the most urgent need to go home. It was a nauseous longing never experienced before. This was a busy crofting homestead and children's nonsense was not pandered to but such was my misery over the next few days, I was sent off home on the bus, but for that day only. Dinah had no daughter of her own and made much of us when in Scullomie and well she knew, my mother needed a break from the demands of her by then five children. Sandra would be 12 and opted to stay at Farr Senior School, despite her good brain and flying pass of the qualifying exam. I was nine and yet to prove my prowess or make my choices. Magnus was six, Muriel five, and Neil two years old, a handful that was thought nothing of, indeed, our mother would have liked another child, but Dad said, enough is enough, probably after battling with Neil's wilfulness, something he never had to do before, the years bringing a leniency and older children, especially me, spoiling the youngest child. I didn't give this favour to Muriel, yet she says I was very good to her and today we have a close relationship, though nothing could be closer than the bond formed between her and Magnus, formed as children and stays strong.

When I arrived home, I was greeted by an empty house, an eerie experience. Searching about I eventually saw figures working in the fields close to the shore. Long before I reached there, a black spot in the distance started racing towards me. The minute I flung my arms round his neck I knew it was not home I missed. It was Rex. I spent the day with him and happily caught the bus back to Scullonie. I never again experienced the debilitating homesickness suffered by some of my siblings as I headed towards years of living in other people's homes, learning how to fit in, and experiencing the excitement of coming back to that precious sanctuary that remained 'home' long after I married at nineteen and delighted in creating another ambience that would eventually be called home by many a stranger who walked through its portals to call out, 'We're home again!' Not we're back, but we're home, and it warmed the cockles of my heart to know they felt that way in a Guest House many hundreds of miles from their own homes.

But all was not well with my acquisition of Rex. This boisterous and clever dog's freedom on the hills with me gave him the notion it was I and I alone he must answer to. He took to gathering a small flock of our hens and bringing them to the green in front of the house. The cockerel took extreme exception to this interference and tackled the dog. The spirited spat between cockerel and dog was entertaining and as the dog attempted to harm only a cockerel that could well defend itself, no one bothered, laughing at their antics as often as not. But when I was at school, Rex got bored and took to herding other people's hens. That was a different story.

'Please, Rex,' I pleaded. 'You can't do that. And you have to answer when Mam calls you.' It made no difference. Then he sealed his fate by going to the Overside and herding sheep. He never harmed any but would not come back when called. As time passed, I cajoled and pled with him to see sense as I would soon be leaving home for five days at a time after passing my qualifying exam. He didn't listen. Soon the day dawned when my father took out the car, put Rex in the back seat beside me and we headed to Dalcharn, a hamlet close to Scullomie,

Without a tear shed I handed over the dog to Danny to train as a working collie, seeing he had such an interest in the coming and going of sheep. I was totally broken hearted but it had to be done. No tantrums or shedding of useless tears. 'You'll upset your mother,' my father said. 'You have to learn,' my mother warned. Had they not cared, they would have done what so many others did at that time. Taken the dog out and shot him.

Rex was very happy in his new home. He was treated as a valued family pet as well as a clever and keen working dog and I could still visit him every summer. Each time I did, he got very confused and followed me for about a quarter of a mile as I headed back to Scullomie. Then he would stop. He just sat there and watched me, as I walked backwards ever so slowly, until I lost sight of him. I suppose today the experience would be called character building.

We saw our cousins often and I heard about Rex all the time, but they were all older boys and loved to tease, so some of the things I heard were at times alarming until an adult cuffed the antagonist. 'Take no heed of him. The dog certainly never did such a thing!'

This was a hard lesson for a 12 year old to learn: be careful what you love. It can be taken away from you. I had loved Rex with every fibre of my being.

And so with my next dog.

Chapter 9

'The dog that trots about finds a bone.'

Golda Meir

Canine Capers

Seven years after giving up Rex, I was back to wanting a cat, preferably a kitten, but a cat would do, any cat.

Did I mention I married a dog man? Well, there was no way I was going to get a cat past him, especially when backed up by his Uncle Jock in their belief that a cat was an unnecessary addition to any household, in particular this house we now shared. So no cat then. Glen, his collie dog, was perfectly capable of keeping vermin at bay. So no excuse either!

But I was a new bride. It shouldn't be that difficult. I was even prepared to adjust my needs, so, in the spirit of compliance, 'What about a dog then, a wee tiny puppy that won't grow any bigger than a cat?'

When I first met Himself, his family had a big, black and white smooth-haired collie called Roy. Roy was lovely and never abused any herding instinct, had no tendency to disobey and was a much loved family pet, but getting on in years so by the time we married, Roy was gone. There was no cat with only Himself's younger brother, Roddy, having a passion for cats. So I thought I was on to a winner when I said, 'It would be fantastic to get a dog.' No response. Then a long stare. Had I said that to my mother or father, I would be pounced upon immediately and told, 'We are not getting a dog,' and I would know where I stood. But this living in each other's pockets, virtual strangers, considering our few meetings before marriage, was new to me. Exciting? Yes. Easy? No! I had yet to learn the signals. Even the rules of engagement were totally different, when he first put a ring on my finger 10 months before our October wedding.

In our young days, couples met in groups far more often than as an item. If the attraction was strong enough, we danced together but meetings were surrounded by others during dances, ceilidhs, concerts, cinema, and the occasional meal out. The old matriarchs who guarded the doors of the dance halls kept an eagle eye on any comings or goings, but with the excuse of no conveniences inside most of the old wooden halls, their job was made doubly difficult!

'I need a pee!' became the passport to all sorts of elicit adventures.

With cars being a luxury few could afford, buses were the main transport, hence the tendency to spread one's friendships into a very wide circle, and the craic on bus trips was a vital part of bonding in any growing friendship. Then, at dances, the stationery bus because a great venue for partying, until one of our self-appointed guardians marched out and asked us what we thought we were up to. They had unimaginable authority when you think of it!

'Get back inside that hall, or your parents will know about this,' was no idle threat. Try that today and see the mouthful you'd get from a 16 year old, and just as likely the parents would say, 'Mind your own business.'

Any alcoholic drink that had passed round was quickly shoved back into a male pocket, but our high spirits were kept up as we obeyed the command. They were not the type of women you disobeyed and sometimes your antics reached the ears of your parents before you got out of bed the next day. Once telephones were installed, tales reached home before you made your weary way, usually in the wee small hours of the morning, dances known to go on until an early rising cock crowed. Sandra and I and my friend Audrey dubbed our mother, Philip Marlow, after the detective series on TV, such was her ability to suss out what we got up to.

We laughed a lot, and probably because we didn't live in each other's pockets, there was no tendency for the meanness that crept into lives much later, driving me to spend more and more time with my horses. It was either them or the nearest psychiatrist!

Ways were found to be together as a couple, but in truth, meeting only once a week, twice maybe, and at times not even as often as that. The telephone became a valuable communication tool, for the few who had phones, with telephonists perfectly well aware the strength of a relationship. In Kirtomy, the day was now gone when our close friend, Betty, more like an older sister to us children and a cherished companion to our mother, raced down from her home where the village telephone was housed, to pass on an urgent message from our father when he came into the port of Scrabster. By the time I went to Miller Academy, a telephone had been installed in that cold and barely used room of mixed memories, but that did not stop me from sitting in the cold, lost in our conversation, until suddenly, the familiar voice of the telephonist interrupted the call.

'Your father is wondering if you're ever going to come off that phone?' So you can imagine how pleased he was when I told him we were getting engaged and not too long afterwards, at the age of 19 years, I was walked down the aisle by a father with a satisfied smile on his face. In his speech, he told everybody, 'I'm looking forward to phoning home without having to ask the telephonist to get that pair off the line.'

The real important things in life were not discussed at any length, just an idea you knew what each other wanted, and you went for it. That's when you found out that what you thought was a great idea, your partner had quite a different view. How the majority of us clocked up long, and in the main, very happy marriages, I'll never know!

With having an older sister, I was lucky, getting out into social circles that parents no longer wished to be part of, Sandra always including me into her group of friends, adding to the mix my two close friends, Donella and Audrey. But many a place neither of us would have got to without Betty. Our parents trusted her implicitly and she became my chaperone, someone who allowed you all the fun you wanted but you did not play silly games with her and when you wanted a pee, I can assure you, all you got was a pee! She, as with so many of the women then, never needed the stimulation of alcohol to have a great time, and to this day, I do believe a drop has never passed her lips. Whereas most of our friends experimented with the different drinks on offer, and I often think, what a blessing it was we did not have the temptation of drugs as young people have today. We never saw alcohol inside the homes except on New Year's day in Kirtomy, and what a great time people had passing one small whisky glass round for each of the men to take a sip from, and each ensuring their expensive and precious bottle of whisky lasted for the duration of that night. Getting in the bottle, really meant exactly that. With reminiscing and camaraderie accompanied by good food, New Year's Night was an occasion to enjoy. Never once did I see anger exchanged on these nights in Kirtomy, a 'dry' village that attracted revellers from villages round about, if they could get their hands on a vehicle, and that essential bottle, without which no man would step over a door!

It was Betty's total approval of Himself that gave him the key to being accepted into our family, where his fit was at times better than my own. My mother never, ever asked him, 'What are you thinking of, doing that?' as she did me, and once you opted to put a wedding ring on your finger, you made your bed and you lay in it without her interference. My father, of course, left needful interferences to the good offices of our mother when we flexed our wings, but we knew exactly where his backing lay, and despite his jovial good nature, not one of us would have defied him. He was a man of considerable standing in the community and I was proud to be known as, 'Magnus Bain's daughter,' even when it left my own identity much lower down the scale. The earliest compliment I got came after I dared to stand up for the rights of the underdog, at a local public meeting, an anonymous postcard coming, merely stating, 'Good for you. You're your father's daughter!' I never showed it to him or told him. He would not have approved anonymity, but I was chuffed, and no doubt emboldened!

By the time I married, my mother had another terrier called Brea who produced puppies soon after our wedding. Sandra picked the runt of the litter and I chose the cheeky one, named him Roxy, went to see him as often as possible, then casually dropped into the conversation, 'This dog, the one I told you about a while back, will soon be ready.' You would think I had dropped a bombshell! It got his attention, for sure. Pity is I never got it when I should have.

'What dog?' Food stopped, half way to mouth. 'Ready for what?'

'To come here, of course.' Not a good start.

'This is not our house. You can't take a dog here.' Himself, who had not earned this highly acclaimed moniker in those early days, got back to the job in hand; his dinner! If any came to the house and asked for Himself, it was Jock they were looking for. But my new husband's attitude soon softened, seeing my stricken face. 'You'll have to talk to Jock.'

This turned out to be far from an 'Ask your father,' situation.

Jock and I got on great, which was not what was prophesied by the villagers upon hearing where we intended spending our married life. My mother was quietly warned how hard it would be for a young girl to stay with this elderly confirmed bachelor, whose reputation for sternness and frugal living went before him along with the knowledge, he stuck to the letter of the law. I never found him anything but straight, generous with his time and his crofting skills, and sympathetic when things went wrong. Growing up in a big family, you learned to make the best of what was on offer and we were brought up to have huge respect for our elders. Jock quickly got over his first introduction to me when I waltzed into his bachelor pad, kitted out in mini skirt and stiletto heels, without a clue as to how a sheep spent its days. Taking an immediate liking to Glen helped, and Jock's stories fascinated, on the occasions I sat by his fire, persuaded into trying his occasional favourite tipple, a shot of whisky with a splash of sherry. The glasses were a joy to the eye, twisted stems, tiny goblets, soft shades of wine, very old and fine as were many of the pieces, clocks and lamps with a delicate beauty, placed on an old dark sideboard with crystal and etched glass displayed in an antique cabinet of similar dark wood.

Newly married with no employment, and no baby on the way to excuse such a state, having to give up my job as assistant manageress in Bettyhill Hotel when I married, I spent a lot of time learning the culinary arts, in particular baking, so Jock became a willing guinea pig. In time he showed me some of his own gastronomic delights. He was a dab hand at making rhubarb jam and the smell of his soups made your mouth water. His living room was large, with the small scullery and small bedroom close by, what we knew in Kirtomy as a closet; today a closet would be a walk-in wardrobe.

We shared a bathroom with a massive Victorian bath I could stretch out in and disappear from all my troubles, most of which I created for myself.

Himself had built us a brand new kitchen leading off the cosy sitting room which was our domain. We ate our food off an old Welsh dresser until he made us a table with that much sought new fabric, red Formica! We had one of the two front upstairs bedrooms, overlooking that wonderful view but close to the hay fields where every summer the corncrakes constant calling near drove me insane. Jock used the other room to store a fascination of trunks and no doubt some junk, but also a stack of genuine antiques. The small bedroom to the back, I was allowed to do up as a single so my best friend Audrey, and Neil, my young brother could come and stay. No one else qualified! And anyway, there's nothing like a spare room to stomp off to when you're getting to know each other.

Like many of the old stone-built crofting houses, no matter the size, the windows were small and there were few with back doors, buildings cleverly located to benefit from the sun and avoid the prevailing winds. We shared the front access and I had the wit to wait some time before persuading Jock that maybe the porch was not quite the best place to store the sheep food when he had plenty of outhouses. This was so effortlessly agreed, I was sure he'd easily approve a companion for Glen, that being my trump card. How wrong was that!

'A terrier!' He looked at me sternly, as if he hadn't really looked at me before. It was a hard stare. 'You can't take a terrier here, Lassie.' That softened the blow. My father called all women of which he was fond, Lassie, regardless of age.

'If you want a dog, it will have to be a collie.' He then muttered more to himself, 'Why would anyone want a terrier?'

I was taken aback. My mother's first terrier, Freuchie had been a very special dog, unbelievably clever, a close companion for all the family and a special friend of the young children next door. We still had him when I left home, after Miller Academy, for the Sutherland Technical College to do a business course, my phone calls home full of enquiries about Freuchie. My mother's generosity in pocket money spent as often as not on gifts for her and the dog.

Arriving home at the end of one term, my first thoughts were of the dog. 'Where's Freuchie?'

99

My mother's face was a sea of misery. 'He was killed Joan, on the road, running to meet the school car.'

I stood there stunned before throwing myself down on the nearest chair and sobbed, a depth of pain cutting much deeper than when Rex had been taken from me. Such a display was a rare sight and my younger siblings looked on open mouthed, but our mother sped them out of the room. 'Leave her. Just leave her. Off out, all of you.'

Eventually I heard the sad tale. Not only did our own children see the accident, but Ena next door's children who adored the dog were witnesses. The youngest boy, Andrew, under school age, stayed with my mother when the others were told, they must go to school regardless. They were stricken with grief, especially Muriel who treated the dog like a baby, that first day especially, but things were different then. And my mother wanted the privacy to grieve in peace. The dog was her shadow all his life. The moment he noticed she was not in the house, he traced her to wherever she was in the village, at times a good long walk away.

Andrew could not be consoled, asking 'Malie, Malie. Why did Hecky kill Ookie?'

My mother held him tight, trying to explain. 'The dog ran...' but the child looked at her in bewilderment, 'Ookie not a dog.' He then shook his head and cried, 'Ookie is... just Ookie. Ookie is Ookie...not a dog!'

That said it all. And now I was faced with a man who could not have known terriers and did not like them at all.

Jock had many reasons for not wanting another dog. He had Glen, his companion and a working sheep dog, but he had a much more ominous reason to add weight to his aversion. He set about ensuring no terrier would cross over his threshold. 'Do you know that if that terrier took Glen away to help him round up sheep, the terrier would tear the bellies out of the sheep.' I looked on aghast. 'And do you know that once blood is tasted, you'll never stop them and that would mean they would be hunted down and shot…like a dog!'

I was too shocked to raise a smile at the analogy.

I cajoled, made ardent promises, then took the law into my own hands. With heart in mouth I arrived with the puppy. On a trial basis. How could they refuse me that.

Little did I know I was bringing into my life an animal who knew exactly what his rights were, and how to exert them!

Chapter 10

*'The fabled musk deer searches the world over for the source
of the scent that comes from itself.'*

Ramakrishna

Deer Oh Deer

Roxy was tiny, ivory coloured with two coal black
eyes, and a jet black nose, both ears folding forward, and I
absolutely adored him. I couldn't push my luck by suggesting
he share our bedroom so his basket was tucked in by the side of
the sitting room fire, and a hot water bottle placed under his
blanket. We slept above, and there wasn't a cheap all night.
What a little angel, I thought.

My heart swelled with the need to be with him, but
from the moment he came into the house, he made it his
mission to spend as much time with Himself as was possible.
Himself resisted the overtures because this was not going to
work out. As Roxy got a little bigger, activities about the croft
fascinated him. If he was left behind, he would leap into a
window to search frantically and howl mournfully before
retiring to his basket with paws over his nose. His first black
mark was scratching the mahogany table we had painstakingly
chosen from the most expensive shop in Caithness,
Mackenzie's, my father guiding us towards all his favoured
stores, insisting if you buy good, you buy well. The young
puppy skidded off the table leaving scratch marks. He then did
exactly the same in the bedroom, marking a mahogany dressing
table, my pride and joy, leaping to the window to see why
Himself had left without him. Nothing barred his way when it
came to keeping a check on the man he had formed such an

attachment to, with no sign of encouragement – that I could see.

One very snowy winter's morning, my husband introduced me to one of the hidden secrets he indulged in…but only occasionally, the risk being very high. It didn't get my approval, but what difference did that make. He didn't stop me from doing what I wanted and in the spirit of appreciating freedom, I returned the compliment. His was a dangerous pastime. But only the physically fit could indulge when it came to walking for miles and miles in hill territory in the hope of carrying back the ill-gotten gain. It was in later years that others took to the roads with search lights, killing indiscriminately, giving the 'one for the pot' mentality of the traditional poacher reason to distance themselves from such practice.

In the early morning darkness he headed out to the hills, for miles, hoping to take down a beast for the family table. It was poaching. But venison was prized and not available to the likes of us, a deer rarely seen by the roadsides like herds are today. Sensible men took the odd one, never selling any part of it, walking great distances and carrying back the animal on their shoulders along with the weight of the rifle that took the animal down, as well as the necessary hot flask and piece bag. This was before a new generation came along with the intention to make money out of such pursuits, and certainly not walking far if they could help it, killing indiscriminately animals from herds skirting the roadsides in their bid to find food as their habitat receded, forestry taking over their ancient tracks, and deer fences sprouting up all over the place.

Many miles out into the snow-covered hills, my man picked up what he was looking for. He quietly stalked his quarry for at least another mile before crawling on his belly to a hillock and getting the animal, a beauty he said, in his sights. Perfect. Gun raised and ready to press the trigger, he felt the hairs on the back of his neck rising. He was being watched. Being caught could mean a prison sentence, and without a doubt a criminal record and the loss of your job. Not something you want at any age but at 28 years, he was determined to avoid such a blight on his character.

He lowered the gun and slowly looked round. Nothing. But he knew he was watched. A flicker, just a tiny movement several yards behind him. He couldn't believe his eyes. Roxy was sitting in the snow, only his black eyes and button black nose visible in the whiteout.

'Roxy?' he whispered in disbelief. The puppy surged forward with a yelp of excitement. That's all it took to spook the trio of hinds he had stalked for the best part of a day.

It had been long after Himself left for the hill I gave in to Roxy's persistent howling and let him out into the garden. Then he vanished, me searching in the snow all day, by night time giving up all hope of seeing the puppy again. I was desolate.

The hunter arrived back very late after trudging miles through the snow, tired and empty handed. Out of his Donkey jacket pocket he produced the missing pup. He was so utterly shocked such a tiny creature could stalk him for hours, he never expressed a word of regret at not bringing back meat for the larder. I had reason to give the mutt one of Jock's hard stares, but was too overjoyed to care about anything except for his survival.

When I set out to visit friends, Roxy whined to be carried and I, soft mug, popped him into the wicker basket I had tucked him into when he first arrived, too small then to walk from my end of Melvich into the heart of Portskerra. This habit made it frustratingly difficult to persuade him to accept a lead. He would throw himself down on the road, on his back, and howl, me trying to cajole him into walking. The minute I pulled on the lead, interested passers-by accused me of abject cruelty. One day a car stopped and offered to take the charming little dog off me as he was obviously so unhappy. He was having a laugh. He could walk for miles and miles through snow, never mind a soft grassy verge in those days before Melvich sported a pavement and the street lighting totally spoiled the intensity of starlit nights with a full moon shining over the Halladale river, the most romantic of settings to sit and enjoy a deliciously cooked venison dinner…when you could get venison!

From the day of his marathon trek to the hill, dog and man sealed a growing bond and Roxy became a highly independent member of our family, taking off to see his selected friends whenever it came up his back. I had to fit in with his lifestyle.

I was asked to help out at the local Hotel that season, when both Audrey and I cocked a snook at our prospective careers in the civil service. We had gone to college together, became true friends and shared the same work at Dounreay until the red tape got us down. We upped sticks for more interesting ways to earn our crust. I had a great notion to enter into the hospitality industry taking on a receptionist's job at Bettyhill Hotel. My mother and my fiancée were not in the least impressed with this decision despite being promoted to its first under Manageress at the tender age of 18 years. But, when I married I was out of a job! Management was expected to remain single and live on the premises. Being out of work was not a big deal in those days, but being of an independent nature, I wanted to earn money. So, an eye-opening stint at the Melvich hotel beckoned, assured it was management work that turned out to be no such thing, but far more fun and far more harassing, chasing around like a mad thing, learning to serve table and see to the house, management not being one of their needs, I was told by a Manageress who, to me who had come from an exceptionally well-run hotel, felt she didn't have much of a clue how to hold on to staff, know who was working where, or inform staff of the needs of the guests. But being a dogsbody appealed to my lively nature and the meagre wage allowed some pin money to appease!

Roxy was not amused to see me leave early each morning, and no matter how often I said, 'Jock, will you pop in and let Roxy out at least an hour after I've gone,' hoping when he felt the need to take to the road, he would just go up the road and play with Rhoda's new kitten, they being tremendous friends playing games that brought chaos to her home. But no, he started to arrive at the Hotel, much to my embarrassment. Rhoda's was not far away and I'd rush him down there, but one day, he didn't suss me out, finding the cook instead. Thus began an instantaneous and mutual love affair. He had another convert. She'd hide him in a cupboard with a bone, walk him in the large vegetable garden. She'd send down titbits to him when he chose not to bother calling that day. He never cared much for food and remained skinny all his life, long legged, always ready for the road. A bit like myself, except I liked my food!

When the cook retired she got herself a terrier as similar to Roxy as she could find, but I doubt it would be possible to get the same characteristics in any other dog.

It was a busy hotel and particularly so during the hunting, fishing seasons. The estate house, Bighouse, was not favoured for staying in when the owners, Mr & Mrs MacFarlane of MacFarlane & Lang biscuit company arrived with their fishing party. They, like so many others of their ilk, preferred to stay in the Hotel.

One morning I was serving their table when I picked up on an animated conversation. They were discussing their water bailiff almost catching a pair of reprobates poaching on the river the night before. My heart began to miss a beat. I rushed off to the kitchen and picked up Mrs MacFarlane's porridge, and a jug of cream. My ears twitched as I hurried to hear more. I heard enough to know who the two miscreants were.

The night before, Himself had headed off to pick up a friend, both keen to get a fish – you never tempted fate by calling the fish a salmon – for the pot. A few hours later, I was wakened by this exhausted man collapsing on the bed, his hand dripping blood. They had been seen on the river and in making an arduous escape, he had badly cut himself. It didn't stop him from going out to work that morning, but the fear always was, did the bailiffs recognise the poachers?

I was about to find out, my eyes anywhere but on the plate of porridge I was placing down in front of Mrs MacFarlane. Suddenly, I felt a hand firmly grip my wrist and turn it so that the porridge that was about to slide off the plate into her lap was placed safely. She gave me a long, steady, stare. I think she knew, but we heard nothing more about it.

My time at the Hotel was short, but interesting, as I succumbed to the lure of the secretarial work back at the local Atomic Station at Dounreay, gaining back the gold star I'd lost when opting for the best fun I ever had associated with work. It's little wonder I ended up persuading youngsters to choose the tourism sector, through helping to build a hospitality degree, knowing they could hit on one of the most fulfilling careers to follow, especially now with all the opportunities around that did not exist in my time. My mantra: go for it!

But, what to do about Roxy?   Other workers' dogs were happy to wait for their owners to come back home. Ours never did. By now he was 'ours' except when he was doing wrong, which was often, then he became 'your' dog.

It was another six years before our son Neil was born, and by then my failures with the dog gave me a better understanding of some of the necessities when bringing up a child, believing as I did in freedom of choice, and seeing corporal punishment as no way to exhort obedience. My father once said, 'You're too hard on that boy.' Was I, I wondered, by demanding standards? Then I remembered the bother Roxy was constantly getting me into and thought, no I'm not! I was sure I wasn't and despite our son's high spirited scrapes, he still grew up with a great care for others, and animals too, and had the sense to bring home a girl, our much-loved Katrina, with similar cares, and they're bringing up their two children in a way that gladdens my heart. You should see the discipline she maintains over their Labrador, and it's all the better for it. But she had two children to practice on before the dog.

I think I was better at bringing up a child, not dogs, or cats, especially black and white cats!

Chapter 11

*'The concept of two people living together for
25 years without a serious dispute suggests a lack of
spirit only to be admired in sheep.'*

A. P. Herbert

A Sheep's Revenge

It didn't take this tiny puppy long to have Jock eating
out of his paw, or he out of Jock's hand as he joined him every
morning to share the fried breakfast Jock indulged in, the
tantalising tang of sausage, bacon and black pudding wafting
into our quarters, enticing Roxy through to where he was
warmly welcomed by both Jock and Glen.

Glen was a playful dog and they had great fun, yet
never in all his years did they run away together, or disturb
sheep. Roxy's other best friend was the daughter of Bimbo, the
name I gave a pet sheep Jock took into the garden to get fresh
grass to bring on her milk. Roxy and the lamb had frantic
games of chase, hide and seek, and King of the Castle. He was
out there every morning the minute the door opened looking
for his woolly friend.

After Bimbo was deemed fit to go back out onto the
croft with her lamb, I heard loud screams coming from the side
of the house. Rushing out I found Bimbo in a right strop,
boxing the living daylights out of the young puppy. She must
have had enough of this alien friendship. A sheep can throw a
right tantrum with a head as hard as ebony to back up any
angst. Never being used to croft animals, I was wary of the
sheep but rushed to rescue the puppy. I knew she could kill

him.   Thankfully, the screams I added to the melee brought
Jock to the rescue.

He grabbed Roxy, but all the sympathy I got was,
'There's no bones broken, he'll be sore for a while. But it's a
good lesson to learn. That will keep him away from sheep for
the rest of his life.' And it did. He never played with the lamb
again, keeping well out of Bimbo's way. However, when in
Kirtomy where we often stayed, home still being where the
heart was, he and Brandy would take to the hills on their own
and worry my mother who was convinced, if seen by a crofter,
they would be shot. Or she would get some horror story of
them chasing a whole flock of sheep over the cliffs. If there
was a worst case scenario, my mother had it played out in her
mind in the hope of avoiding it becoming a fact.

There was no end to her imagination of things that
could go wrong. The dogs always came home in the most
terrible state, caked with mud, covered in twigs and heather,
skulking round corners and creeping in the door, guilty as sin.
It was obvious they were down holes and up to all sorts of no
good, but never was a spot of blood found on them. Roxy was
easy to bath, despite his protests, but Brandy was a big dog and
it was better to let the mud dry and brush it out of his beautiful
rusty coat. They could not be stopped from these adventures,
Neil administering terrible threats to his dog, my
admonishments having no impact whatsoever upon Roxy. His
trips to Kirtomy came to a stop much to his disgust, car travel
being high on his entertainment agenda. Our car was tiny and
the dog easily stood on the back seats with paws on the front
seats, balancing perfectly while he watched the road as eagle-
eyed as any driver. When I drove, he barked soundly in my ear
each time a vehicle hove into view, yet he felt no need
whatsoever to bark a warning when Himself was at the wheel.

Then, sometime after the poaching episode, Roxy
went missing. I was heartbroken. Despite being difficult to
train to the lead, we walked the main road through Melvich,

and all round Portskerra, having many friends to visit in both villages. His favourites were not necessarily my friends but older women he had a great rapport with, so he took to visiting them on his own. He quickly made a friend of both mobile butchers, and could foretell their coming long before they drove into the village. When I was working, he would be waiting for them at Rhoda's and then at Shonag's, down Portskerra. I did keep an eye on him, but he was elusive and a free spirit, more like a cat which I could relate to so easily.

At that time, Himself was on shift work at Dounreay, and not interested in New Year revelries the night the young dog went missing after I headed to Kirtomy, leaving Roxy with my in-laws. Rhoda's youngest daughter, Georgie, telephoned on New Year's Day, and into the well-wishing conversation I asked, 'How is Roxy behaving?'

Silence. Then, 'You've got Roxy,' she said.

'No. He's with you. I left him at your house.' They were a big family, Georgie, Barbara, and their sister Dolly with her husband Donnie, all living there at that time, all of whom would have been at their work, and Rhoda was profoundly deaf, so mistakes easily made with a dog who came and went between our houses, just as it suited. On the rare occasion Roxy was ticked off by Himself, the dog took it so much to heart, the minute he got out, he was off up the road to throw himself under their sideboard where he would wail all night if Donnie did not spend considerable time commiserating with him. Our homes were about a quarter mile apart, along the main road or through the hills. Roxy didn't mind which way and was so good at the green cross code, our local policeman said it was amazing to watch him, especially when big lorries had him skedaddle into an adjoining field. He knew all about the power of large vehicles. Donnie always took him in his lorry, sometimes for long trips, which the dog loved, devoted as he was to Donnie until he made the unintentional miscalculation of introducing the dog to their new born son by showering the baby with unadulterated delight. They had moved to a house in Portskerra and when visiting the baby for the first time, Roxy was with me, excited he was going to see Donnie, his next best person after Himself, not forgetting his trio of old ladies, the paper boy, Tommy, who was a special favourite, Jock, and my mother and no doubt others. I was just his carer, devoted to his needs, there for him whatever the situation. A good servant!

Donnie picked up young David, swaddled as babies were at that time, swayed him back and fore in his arms, 'Look at this, Roxy. See what I have,' as he fussed and petted their beloved son.

Roxy was unimpressed. Donnie doubled his efforts.

Roxy turned his back. That was it. For Roxy the situation was non-negotiable. Donnie lost all favour, forever.

Soon Donnie and Dolly, and their firstborn, moved to Livingstone, so the rift was never mended. This did not bode well for my hopes to have a child Roxy would love, and we did plan having one, hopefully more than one, some day.

And now this independent canine had disappeared. For a fortnight into the New Year, there was no letting up in our search for the dog. It was before Donnie's construed betrayal, and none of Roxy's usual haunts proved fruitful. I was devastated. Then my cousin who drove a mobile grocery van along the coast, told me one of his customers, an elderly lady who lived with her husband in Strathy West, said she had a lovely new dog and needed to buy food for him. He arrived out of the blue, a very young dog, settled in by their fire and was so happy with them. He loved walking, racing ahead of them and bobbing up to make sure they followed. He was giving them so much pleasure. 'How could anyone throw out such a lovely animal? A Christmas present gone wrong,' she sighed to Angus.

'How can it be Roxy, they live miles away.' It was an impossibility.

'I'd check it out if I were you.' I was not hopeful when I followed the advice. Heart in mouth, I drove there and knocked on a door I had never before seen. A ferocious barking came from within. I knew that bark!

The door opened cautiously, and a lovely grey haired woman held the squirming dog in her arms. He was not yet fully grown and quite small but he wriggled free and gave me the most heart-warming welcome. Nobody could explain how he got there, but Sandra and her husband, Malcolm, lived in Strathy then, less than a mile away, and Roxy came with me on my many visits to their home in the old manse. Apparently, the puppy followed Malcolm to Strathy West one day when he did some work there. Whatever was in the young dog's mind, he did not go near Sandra's, with her new baby, Lorna, getting all the attention, instead choosing to be king pin in someone else's child and animal free home.

The woman loved that dog, and I felt dreadful, but Roxy made it quite clear, his holiday was over, and he would go home now. And I couldn't part with him.

Despite Himself's determination that Old Jock, the handyman at the hotel had been talking rubbish, after four years of living with his Uncle Jock, the notion came upon him to put his skills as a joiner to good use and so began the two-year build of The Sheiling, the house dubbed The Tardis by visitors as in time we grew it into a Guest House. Self-build, despite much help from David, his entrepreneurial brick-laying friend, takes time and all during the long build, Roxy was Himself's constant companion.

One lovely summer day, as my hard-working husband plied the trowel to the brick wall he had half built, Roxy took it into his head to relieve boredom by chasing this particularly noisy old tractor making heavy weather of its frequent trundling up and down the main road. No amount of calling would stop his fun as he raced towards the lumbering vehicle to snap at its wheels, much to the consternation of the driver.

Suddenly the tractor stopped. The driver got off, shouting at the dog as it sprinted back up the hill, waiving his fists in anger as he raced after the dog, furious at the constant interruptions.

Himself, being totally unable to control the dog, had no intention of letting the driver know he was anywhere in the vicinity. So he hid behind the wall. He prayed he would not be found out, but once committed to hiding, he had to stay there, listening with eyes tightly closed, face down, hoping the dog had taken to the hills. The shouting stopped and he opened his eyes. There was Roxy, lying flat out beside him, paws as ever over his nose, one eye watching him with a look as if to say, 'Are you going to defend me or not when that madman gets us?' Fortunately, the sound of the tractor spluttering back into life resolved the situation. Roxy was on another of his many warnings.

Neil was born the year we moved into the new house and I feared the dog would not take kindly to such an insult, having taken to his new home with relish. You could tell; he helped to build it! But I need not have worried about this new squirming, yelling, squeaking, smelling addition to the household. The dog accepted the baby without fuss, the only incident happening when the district nurse called, and I left the room to make tea, the baby lying on a rug in front of the fire with the nurse looking on. Roxy had not appeared to be in the least bit interested.

Nurse Mackay bent down and put out her hands to pick up the baby. Roxy moved over and snarled. She knew him. This was not like him at all, so she warily tried to pick up the baby. This time he barked. I rushed back and the dog retreated, wagging his tail. She could have the child, but only if I were there. Roxy never bothered much with our son as he grew; no jealousy, no fuss, a newcomer to the home, but he was ours, therefore acceptable. He had the smell of Himself about him, so must be acceptable.

We had no pavements or street lighting, and the road then was fairly narrow, yet when Neil started school at the age of five, there being no nursery or pre-school opportunities in those days, no parent walked their child to school. The traffic did not tear along the road, except for the odd boy racer who soon got his ears bashed, if not by the local copper or a parent, then certainly by anyone else who felt justified. So, after the first day, Neil walked the mile to school by himself, being just outside the requisite area to get a lift in the school car. I don't recollect being particularly worried. It was normal, and nobody seemed to talk about child abduction then. Tommy, Roxy's much-loved paper boy, lived even further from the school and walked every day, doing his paper round en route home each afternoon and every Saturday. Later, his brother Angus also walked every inch of the way to school, and thought nothing of it, but in time, such distances were covered by school runs.

But there was one pair of very concerned canine eyes watching my child. They were not Roxy's. Yet our dog took up his stance in a dignified wait, sitting out on the concrete slab housing the sceptic tank, a high point that allowed him see the child making his way home. Roxy then meandered down the driveway to meet Neil at the roadside and walk him back up to the house, wagging his tail, nothing more than that, but he had that contented look on his face that said all is well in my world. By then Roxy had stopped much of his independent lifestyle, continuing to visit Jock, and Rhoda's occasionally, the visit including her elderly neighbour Eanie, but Portskerra no longer drew his interest. He, like me, was settling down to domesticity.

It was then that I discovered a trait in my son that became a self-preservative mechanism, apparently to this day. I was told by one of the people who lived up the road, that from the day the child started to walk to school, the collie dog belonging to the shepherd, Hugh Mower who lived just up the road from us, left his habitual stance in front of his master's house and accompanied my child to school. It was close to a mile in distance.

My friend Joey was another who verified this. Joey was terrified of dogs after a bad experience when a child, though she had a liking for Roxy. When she met Neil coming home, as she often did, the dog would herd him to the inside and make sure Joey walked round both of them! She was quite happy to do this, not entirely trusting the dog, but Spot wouldn't have touched her.

The collie was not often able to meet Neil coming home, but when he could, he would. 'You never told me Spot walks to school with you Neil?' I said after speaking to Joey.

'You never asked.' And that became his standard reply throughout his youth to any accusation of withholding information. According to Katrina, he still does it!

He did eventually tell me that some of the boys at school took to throwing stones at Spot, who eventually took him only as far as the Hotel, and at times would be waiting there to walk him home. Then new people came to the village who became great friends, with four boys of their own. Irene took over the school run and as there was an empty seat in the car, she picked up Neil and the collie's duties came to a halt.

It does make you wonder, just what makes an animal tick!

Chapter 12

*'The crafty rabbit has three different entrances
to its lair.'*

Chinese Proverb

Run Rabbit Run

I probably took Joan, my god-daughter, to Thurso because her mother was looking after Neil, while I shopped for the food needed in my bed and breakfast. I wasn't too serious about this venture into taking money from strangers who opted to stay under our roof, but I stuck with it, though I made sure my friendships, like the one I had with my cousin Pat, my sisters and sisters-in-law, remained an important part of my life, seeing them as often as possible along with the friends made in the village.

As the young child and I drove out of the small town, I mentioned in passing, 'That's the new pet shop, Joan.'

'Can we go and see it?' She was a quiet wee thing, still in the primary school, though feisty when it mattered to her, the youngest in a family of six.

'Sure, why not.' If I had known why not, I'd never have set foot in there, but in we trooped and were immediately drawn to a pen full of tiny, black, very long-eared rabbits. I once asked if I could have a pet rabbit, after watching with envy on a childhood trip to Thurso, the small daughter of my mother's friend, play with a large grey rabbit on a rug in front of the fire. We weren't children encouraged to believe we could get what we wanted although by the time Neil, my youngest brother came along and was taken to Thurso, he near drove our mother insane, not wanting, but demanding that he be given the massive statue of a horse in St John's Square. The days of Jimmy Clachan's horse in the stables at Kirtomy were long gone, but there was still a bit of work for a horse in the village and one was taken from Strathy to do some work. Magnus made great friends with its owner, calling him The Mannie and dogged his footsteps throughout the village. Neil was a lot younger and was convinced the horse in St John's Square would suit his desire to be a cowboy. For him it was that horse; for me, it was that rabbit. I was consumed with desire. I coveted the rabbit. I dreamed about it. And eventually I tentatively asked, 'Can I have a rabbit?'

'There's a hare in the cupboard and you'll get it tomorrow. You'll have to do with that.'

It wasn't quite what I meant. The hare had been hanging upside down for a couple of days, waiting to be skinned and turned into a family roast. We had hare soup the day after it was hung up by my father and had its blood drained to make the soup, a savoury brown dish we all loved as a rare treat. It was not something we talked about as shooting hares was poaching! And my mother did not like being party to anything that flouted the letter of the law. Venison and hare were not a meat seen for sale in the butcher's, more likely to come from a country estate, if you had the right connections and could afford it. Our father shot hare and rabbit, but never deer. He kept his poaching skills for chasing the shoals of fish he seemed to smell in the water before radar gave the boats an advantage not known in the early days of sourcing a catch.

One special day, the whole family lunched in the very posh dining-room of the Royal Hotel at Thurso, that being the place to be seen in those days. The atmosphere was hushed, just the clink of silver on china and quiet footsteps as the busy waitresses went silently about their business on the rich, thick carpeting. In charge was a Head Waiter well known for his lordly stance and his fine opinion of himself. He didn't serve at table, he just stood there, white gloved hands behind his back until his beckoning finger indicated where service was required. He was nicknamed The Penguin and indeed looked like one in his black long-tailed coat and pristine white shirt and white bow-tie.

Discomfort for our mother began with Muriel insisting she wanted to go and see the penguin. It took persistence to shut her up. Then, when Windsor Soup arrived, Magnus got very excited and shouted to everyone, 'Look! We've got hare soup. We got hare soup!'

'I was never so black affronted in all my life,' we heard for some time to come. In truth, family lunches in such prestigious surroundings were few and far between, and you can see why!

As a very small child, after the war when Dad was home for a period of time, he brought back so many rabbits for the table, this delicious meat was added to the list of things my mother didn't want to see again, insisting she would take 'the jaundice' when I first heard her wail, 'If I see another rabbit, it will turn my stomach!'

There was no way I was getting a pet rabbit growing up in Kirtomy. And there was no way I could refuse a small child who turned earnest eyes upon me. 'Can I get one of the little rabbits?' that day I took my Goddaughter to the new pet shop. It would be OK, I was sure, as Pat and I had come home from a hilarious time in Aberdeen, attending a Gaelic Mod with my parents, and in the boot of the car were two large pet rabbits, immediately dubbed Neil and Angus, after two young men we all met at a ceilidh, their wit and entertaining spirits adding to the good time had by all. It was the only time in my life I knew my dignified mother to be thrown out of a public place. One afternoon we went to see the new Bond film, From Russia With Love, and were settling into the film when these two comedians crept in behind us and spent more time making us laugh than watching the film. Eventually, to my mother's utmost horror, the usherette arrived with her torch and demanded our family get out. Not the pair who caused the hilarity, but us. I swore it was my mother's raucous laughter that attracted the attention.

'I have never been so black affronted in all my life,' she admonished, but she saw the funny side, and I knew she had thoroughly enjoyed the laugh with these fluent Gaelic speaking islanders who followed us out and insisted we would all be much better off forgetting the film and finding another ceilidh which was not difficult at an Aberdeen Mod. The rabbits were Pat's gift for the children, but that was some years back and the rabbits were now gone. But their hutch was still there.

I was now drooling over the Rex rabbits and one little black buck was put into a brown paper bag and handed to the waiting child. We bought its food and bedding, then headed out of the shop. Just by the door, Joan stopped. She stood transfixed in front of a cage of piebald mice. There was a baby racing round and round on a wheel. She couldn't take her eyes off it.

'Come on Joan. We need to get that bunny home as soon as we can. What are you going to call him?' I asked, trying to distract her.

'I want that mouse. Please. I don't really want the rabbit.' Joan was always pretty straight with her intentions in life. You knew where you stood with her.

'What? That horrible little creature? Joan, your mother will kill me if I take that thing home. The rabbit is perfect, and she'll love it.'

'I like the mouse best. She'll like it. I know she will.' She was very certain. I was aghast at the thought of returning the rabbit to its cage. And putting this creepy little thing, all sharp nose, beady black eyes and ears like dinner plates with whip-lash tail, into a paper bag and taking it all the way to Armadale went against all my animal-loving instincts. I shuddered. It didn't even look as if it had fur on its body. Who was this child of such weird tastes!

Remembering the day of her Christening, maybe I was a bad influence on her. Church services were held in the Armadale village hall and most of the villagers attended regularly, particularly so to a Christening. It was the year before I married and I, as Godmother, was a bag of nerves as I carried the shawl-wrapped baby to the church. A car drew alongside us, Pat's brother-in-law at the wheel.

'You're awful white looking, Joan,' he observed.

'I'm petrified,' I wailed, still holding the baby, the hall several yards along the road.

'Here,' he said, reaching into the glove box. 'Have a drop of that and you'll be fine.' Shifting the baby I reached over, then got a wallop on my back. 'Are you out of your mind?' Pat was none too pleased that I could succumb so easily to such an offer. 'Go in there with your breath stinking of whisky, and anyway, that's my daughter you have in your arms. Give her to me.'

'No! Don't be silly, I was only joking.' But I wasn't. We quietly sang the hymn, *Yield Not To Temptation*, as we continued down the road, taking a terrible fit of the giggles once we stood in front of the congregation. Inappropriate laughter is a family trait that follows most of us to this day, funerals of the elderly being a real trial. I hope they all laugh plenty at mine as I intend being extremely elderly by the time I get there, growing old with enough courage to give them plenty to laugh about as I depart these earthly constraints!

I was now losing the battle to budge that little madam from her determination to have the mouse. It went into a bag and she doted on it for years until, as an old, old, fellow, it eventually gave up the ghost. In all my frequent visits to her home, I could never take to Thomas – funny name to give a mouse. But her dedication to his welfare was admirable, supported by her mother who shared its caring, and mourned its passing. I was kept well abreast of its activities, whether I wanted to know or not.

As to the little black bunny, rustling about inside its paper bag, I couldn't take it back. So I took it home, not even thinking of the consequences. Neil had a bendy Bugs Bunny toy he was fond of and when the two year old saw the rabbit, he looked at it in wonder and asked 'What's 'at?'

'A rabbit. A little bunny rabbit.' My mind was flying wondering what to do with it, a hunting cat roaming about the house, and a terrier dog that chased and killed rabbits in the wild.

The child looked at me sceptically. 'S'not a rabbit. 'Sa Bendy!' So Bendy the rabbit became. Himself was well out of it, working for weeks away from home, giving up his boring job at Dounreay the minute he finished building our new home, The Sheiling, and with no phone installed, despite doing bed and breakfast, communication was slow. Sandra had an excellent wicker cat basket that served as a safe sleeping quarter for the tiny black bundle. But what about his more basic needs? I hadn't a clue but put down thick newspaper in a corner of the living room and he immediately used it for his toilet but when introduced to the outdoors, he quickly asserted his ability to go in and out as he pleased, with no more use of an indoor toilet. He never ever left these little rabbit droppings anywhere in the house.

Puss-do, the black and white cat Neil got from Connie's mother, quietly accepted the rabbit, never harming it, but Roxy looked on with startled disbelief. I had words with all three, explaining that Bendy was not on the menu. The rabbit took to following the dog about which was not appreciated, the dog taking to skulking under the writing bureau, peering out at Bendy, unable to believe his eyes. Himself started to call the dog Skooker, and Skooker stuck.

One day, not long after the rabbit arrived, with husband at home, we took the chance to lie out on the green at the side of the house and catch some sun. I was keeping an eye on this tiny creature who was stealing hearts, but its size and place in the food chain made it highly vulnerable. That previous Christmas, a trio of identical fluffy stray kittens, along with a smooth-haired grey and white sibling were dumped in the whins behind the house. Puss-do made friends with them and of course, I fed them despite being so wild you could never get a hand near them. Now I was fearful they may think Bendy was an extra special treat.

Sleepily keeping an eye on the rabbit, I heard Roxy return from a run up the hill. He thumped down a tiny baby rabbit right by my nose. I leapt up and shouted, 'Roxy! You horrid dog,' Overtaking full grown rabbits when on walks proved no problem to the dog and calling him back was useless. My distress at hearing the rabbit's scream was met with, 'Well, what do you expect. You wanted a terrier, and he's only following his instincts.'

Roxy took off up the hill again. By now I was sitting up watching Bendy. Within half an hour that dog dumped five tiny dead bodies in front of us. Bendy was not in the least bit interested in the small corpses. He was, as ever, more interested in the movements of the dog. Roxy had never done anything like this before. I knew the female rabbit sometimes make a scrape in the sand where she keeps her kits, and cats can listen for noise, then dig down and take the nest. The safest nests were in the many burrows in the warren half way up the hill behind the house, with some particularly large rabbits romping about. These wild creatures became remarkably tame with little fear of me as I went in and out to the back green.

I was very worried. This seemed a real threat to my newly acquired pet.

Chapter 13

'A great many people now reading and writing would
be better employed keeping rabbits.'

Dame Edith Sitwell

Bunny Business

Life continued with added interest, living alongside one of the first rabbits I knew of that had the freedom to come and go as it pleased. It was some years into the future before rabbits became a fashion fetish with large indoor cages, toys and all the accoutrements for a growing trade filling the shelves of pet stores. But it was all new to me and had come about by default.

The dog, despite that dire warning, never actually touched the rabbit but at times was sore pushed. Bendy grew large, and became quite dominant, at times like a mad March hare, but never ever did he use tooth or claw to a human being. On a cold night Roxy loved to lie right close to the open fire. It was his favourite place, but without preamble, Bendy would come along, push him out, and the dog would retire to under the bureau, while the rabbit stretched out in his place. I soon discovered you could train a house rabbit to be very clean, but fail utterly in controlling his dominant streak with other animals.

He never did droppings anywhere in the house, he never ever chewed cabling, wallpaper or floor coverings. For as long as he lived, he only damaged a carpet once. We left him in the wicker basket in front of the fire one New Year's Eve and were first-footing till all hours. Sleeping late the following morning, when I opened the living room door,

Bendy had escaped from his basket and dashed for the back door. Before I could open it, he flooded the floor, a desperate look on his face. I couldn't believe a rabbit could hold all that liquid and was grateful it was on the tiled back lobby he had lost control. He had almost made it outside!

Going back to the living room, I found the carpet all scraped at the door and a hole in the basket where he had chewed his way out. I felt suitable guilty, but in truth, until I got other rabbits, I didn't appreciate how rare his behaviour was, making Bendy an exceptional house pet.

Although we had moved up to The Sheiling some months before Neil was born, our son spent a lot of time with Jock and his sheep, out on the croft, and where they went, Glen went. I was wary of Glen's reaction to the rabbit but I needn't have worried. They took to each other and all Bendy's life, they played and romped together, the dog chasing the rabbit into bushes and the rabbit pouncing out on the dog.

Lots of families stayed with us then and most were intrigued by the rabbit. Once, a card arrived, addressed to 'The House of the Black Rabbit'. The postman was a special favourite, always coming in with the mail to see if Bendy was about. House rabbits were not known in our circles before the seventies, and many called just to spend some time with him. He didn't take much to do with Puss-do, or her feral friends, but seemed to go in and out with Roxy. Yet, he took extreme exception to guest's dogs and the following extract from *Bye Bye B&B* gives you an insight into the rabbit's temperament.

'Oh, you've got a rabbit,' a rather pernickety lady gasped as she came into the lounge. 'Maybe you should put it back in its hutch. John will be bringing the dog through in a moment.'

I explained that this was our pet, a resident rabbit, and he had never lived in a hutch, the fields and the hills being his territory, where he bossed about a colony of wild rabbits and chose his own doe from amongst them. The house, to which he had access whenever he wished, was his 'hutch'.

'He seldom stays out at night, always keeping roughly to the hours of the dog.'

'A dog? You have a dog as well as a rabbit, living in the house?' She looked quite perplexed.

'Skooker's not at home. He just comes and goes as he pleases, visiting my in-laws. He's visiting his friends at the moment, three elderly ladies he goes to see. He never misses out on a Wednesday, the day the butcher's van is on the go, but he's in here by evening time and funnily enough the rabbit is inclined to come home from the hills then too.'

'But we must be careful our dog doesn't harm the rabbit, mustn't we, John dear?' She patted the couch for John dear to sit down beside her, and pass a wheezing King Charles onto her lap.

Cue the rabbit. He sat staring at them for a time, particularly watching the dog, then as other guests gathered, he approached John dear and his wife, whose name I now forget.

'Oh, isn't he sweet?' she enthused as he allowed himself to be stroked. Then without warning the rabbit got up on his hind legs in a startlingly menacing position and shot out his front paws in boxer style, spitting from the back of his throat. Low guttural growling noises filled the room as sharp claws slashed the air in a very threatening manner. The recipients of this display were no longer amused and John dear was asked to remove their darling dog to the safety of the bedroom. The rabbit and I got looks to match his colour for the rest of the night.

Had I been allowed a rabbit, in a hutch, as a child, I would have better appreciated the character of an animal who became known to the one vet who single-handed ran a practice in Thurso that now takes a very large team of vets, nurses and clerical staff to cope with all the work it takes to keep the area free from farming disasters, and us small animal owners happy. It's a great practice with an excellent reputation, but it was built on the skills and empathy of one of the most respected and hard-working men in the area, Mr Donald McGregor, our local veterinary surgeon.

For a while, when new heating was installed in the school, we had the engineers, two young lads, stay with us and Bendy spent a lot of time with them. I let them use our private sitting-room so they didn't have to mix with guests who only wanted to talk about their holidays and quiz the life out of the boys each evening when the boys just wanted to watch TV.

'Did you know Bendy is crossing the road, going down into the fields over there?' one asked, idly stroking the back of the rabbit as I took their breakfast order.

'Oh, no. I always thought he spent all his time with the rabbits up the back.'

'What's worrying us, we saw a rabbit with myxomatosis down near the river.'

This was dreadful news. I began to watch Bendy and discovered another peculiarity of his. He sat on the middle of the main road, just before the Mail bus from Thurso trundled its slow way through the village towards him. When the bus reached him, he skipped, zig-zagging, up the road in front of it, then veered up our drive. I tried my best to stop him, and was successful in preventing him going over the road to the fields that run towards the river. But, invariably, when I checked about the time the bus was due, there he would be, same carry-on.

One day the bus stopped. Out jumped Hughie Reid, the driver, and chased the rabbit up the road, furious with him. I raced down the driveway to make amends. 'I'm sick of him, and one day he's going to get killed. He's never there in the morning, but as often as not, in the afternoon, there he is, sitting waiting!' Hughie's face was red with exertion and exasperation, a man with unbelievable good nature as he did favour upon favour in his daily trips into Thurso, for any in need and unable to make that trip.

I made my profuse apologies, errant rabbit in my arms, passengers all agog. The road had not been widened then and was far from busy or fast, but he could so easily get killed.

'I like the animal. I don't want to see him hurt, but he's holding me back, and you'll have to keep him in.'

'Impeding delivery of the Royal Mail is a criminal act,' I told the rabbit in no uncertain terms. Like all the mail bus drivers, they knew everyone on their route and Hughie Reid was a fine man. I felt really bad that he should be so hassled by a rabbit.

Not long after that, early one morning, Bendy did not look well. He didn't want to go out. Himself was working at home at the time, and getting a lift to work with his friend, Ronnie, who came in every morning, just to say hello to the rabbit. They were great mates.

'Where's Himself today, then?' Ronnie asked. He was not referring to my husband. For him, Bendy was top dog in the house.

'He's not well, and I am so scared it may be myxomatosis.'

Without more ado, Ronnie said, 'Right, we're taking him to the vet. I'll be straight back for you in half an hour.' He was back in 20 minutes! There followed a journey of terror for me, the quiet rabbit on my knee, the child in the back, and an absolutely furious Ronnie, driving like a maniac whilst cursing the person who brought this heinous disease into our country, and those who spread it. We knew keepers did that deliberately, to get the 'vermin' off the land, keep down the foxes with less to feed on. Today it is a rare sight to see a rabbit bounding by. It took decades to achieve, but well done the keepers, with the rabbits gone, so went many other species that ensured wild life close to our doors in the natural chain of evolution before man's intervention.

The vet confirmed what I believed to be a death sentence. Bendy must be put to sleep. I felt sick to my core as I stood there with him in my arms. It was a minute before I realised Mr MacGregor was talking about the need to know more about this disease, Aberdeen University seriously researching it. He insisted, there is always a chance. There was no cure, nor as I knew, had there been a vaccination at that time that may have given him protection against the worst of the disease.

'I'd like to treat him. But it's the nursing that will matter. I'll give you the medication if you'll do the nursing. It won't be easy, but it's often loving care that brings an animal through a bad time, as much as any medicine.' I was nodding my head, barely able to believe the reprieve. 'To start with he'll get antibiotics by injection, then you must get him to take daily doses by mouth. He'll get very sick, and he'll get tumours all over his body. I'll give you cream for the lumps. Let's see how it goes.'

I couldn't speak. We were all devastated, but I was determined that if there was a chance, Bendy would get it. I made a bed up for him in my sitting room, away from the guests. I got a cat litter tray and put newspapers in it. So many people could not believe the rabbit was ill, my mother and father among them. I kept other visitors away as Bendy soon began to look a sorry sight.

Because I had a blood condition that required twice weekly injections, one of his regular visitors was the district nurse. She kept an eye on him too, and brought him thick incontinent pads so his urine would not affect the tumours that formed on his private parts. Pets now have their own incontinent material, for training purposes and sick animals, but then there were was nothing I knew of, so I was grateful, not just to our local district nurse, but to Dorothy too when she was on duty and sneaked me a pack. I had a cushion with a big button indentation in the middle and this was Bendy's favourite seat, often placed on my knee as he began to get more lethargic and much more petted. Giving him his medication was difficult and I always nursed him wearing a specially bought white coat easily slipped off. I never knew the minute a guest would call me, and hygiene had to be upheld.

One day, without thinking, I put my finger in my mouth with the bright turquoise antibiotic powder still on it. The taste was vile so no wonder Bendy refused it at first. But he had a passion for bananas. When hidden in these, he got his daily dose with no more fuss. He also loved mandarin oranges, would sit on his hind feet, hold a segment in his front paws and let the juice dribble down his chin as he munched away. He loved a cup of tea, with lots of milk and had his own tiny cup. His condition worsened as the weeks went by, despite the constant nursing and medication that the vet continued to provide free of charge. By now we had a car again, so I was mobile, but eternally grateful to Ronnie for all his help.

One day my mother said, 'Joan, that rabbit is going to get better. There's a brightness in his eyes today.' No way, I thought. She's just wishing that. Why she cared, I didn't know and the things he did to her. I'll never forget the day they called to take Neil and me up to Kirtomy and Dad let the rabbit out. He headed for his haunts in the hill and my mother shouted, 'It's OK, I'll get him back in.'

I was in the kitchen, with the back door open and saw her going into the field to pick him up. He moved on up the hill, just a bit. She followed, stretched out her hands, and he hopped on a bit further. Then he waited. She caught up and went to pick him up. He moved on. This was repeated a couple of times more as he enticed her further and further up the hill. I was just about to shout I would get him myself, when she bent down again and he let fly with his back feet. She screamed, though he had not made contact. Then I saw her take a white hankerchief out of her suit pocket; a beautiful navy suit with a lovely white blouse; and start to wipe her face.

She saw me in the doorway and yelled over, 'Just look at what that rabbit of yours did to me!'

Her blouse and skirt were covered in urine as was her face. I didn't know then that spraying is a Lepus defence mechanism! He got such a ticking off when I got my hands on him. It was his answer to being kept in for the afternoon. As a youngster he came to Kirtomy with us but now he was fully grown I was afraid he would sneak out there and get lost. This I could not risk, so he had to stay in.

A couple of days after my mother's positive prognosis, the nurse called. 'Do you know, I think he's improving.' And he was, but when I took him back to the vet to have this confirmed, I said, 'Now he's on the mend, he wants back out to the toilet more than anything. I'd love to let him, as he hates dry food and prefers getting his own, but is it safe?'

'Oh, he's on the road to recovery all right. But, by law, I must tell you that you cannot let a myxomatosis rabbit mix with other rabbits, and spread the disease, even if they are wild, and knowing so little about the disease, we don't know if he is still infectious.'

I couldn't believe my ears. What about people deliberately spearheading the disease? I had to buy him a soft cat harness and lead, and that's how guests arrived at the house to find their hostess for that precious stay, out walking a scabby looking rabbit on a lead! You could tell they wondered what they were coming to!

He romped on the lead without any problem, and taught me so many things about the life of wild rabbits, facts I could verify when Richard Adam's *Watership Down* came out, reading about rabbit toilets and many other traits I was aware of through Bendy. His toilets amazed me. Some on hollowed rocks, others on large tussocks of peat abandoned by the side of the peat-stack, old rabbit droppings visible as he added to the pile. He was always finicky about his food, only wanting to eat greens from the countryside. When he was ill, each time I took my mother to Thurso, we would stop by the roadsides to pick Dandelions, his out and out favourite, starting always with the stem and munching his way up to the flower that would disappear into his mouth as he lay convalescing. Certain flowers from the garden suited him too, especially roses, and many a beauty went down his throat while we waited for the all-clear that would allow him his freedom once again.

Nine long weeks after being diagnosed with myxomatosis, the first ever known pet rabbit to survive the disease romped out the back door and headed straight to the fence that surrounded the house. We watched, holding our breath as he leapt through the wire, fur all restored to a glistening black. The only mark left on him was a small round hole in his ear where two back to back pustules had healed, leaving what looked like a lug hole identification mark.

There was a large wild rabbit grazing outside the fence. Within a minute, they were leaping and dancing in displays I had never seen before.

'Wow!' I said to Himself. 'What a welcome Bendy is getting.' Maybe too much of a welcome as a few tufts of fur began to fly. Several more rabbits were milling about, and there was Bendy's own special doe. Though many had succumbed to myxomatosis during the weeks Bendy was recovering, this particular pale buff rabbit, with a big white star on her forehead was not one of them. He used to bring her to the back door when he was coming in, but the moment I appeared, off she would shoot. He'd watch her run, then look at me as if he couldn't understand why. Other times, looking out the back sitting-room window, there he would be, lying in the shelter of a large whin bush, washing her as she stretched by his side, unaware we spied on their romance. She was now a spectator to the aerobatic display.

'That's what you think,' I was told in a matter of fact voice. 'That's no welcome. That's another buck and they're fighting.'

'What?' I yelled, heading for the door to defend my darling on his first day out. By the time I reached, Bendy was sitting on his back legs, straight as a dye, boxing the air about him, a 'Who dare meddle with my warren,' look on his face. Star was beside him, the rest of the depleted warren hopping about their business.

He was back, the usurper gone. They all knew who was boss!

Chapter 14

'If you keep your feathers well oiled, the water of criticism will run off as from a duck's back.'

Ellen H. S. Richards

Quacking Like A Duck

Though I wasn't allowed a rabbit as a child, we did have ducks as pets. My mother was determined she would rear ducklings, having considerable success with chickens. There was a large park at the back of the house and through it ran a trickle of water, my father broadening out an area that was lovely and muddy, roots growing about it and perfect for ducks. Sandra had a large, waddling, dark coloured duck, with lots of beautiful rich green feathers. We loved that duck as much as Magnus and Muriel loved special hens they picked out as their own, naming them, but I don't remember our duck having a name. Not that she was my duck.

Now and again, balls of yellow fluff suddenly appeared, waddling in line behind the mother duck, but as often as not, she paraded her brood down Merran's brae and took them to the burn. At times she did not bring them all back, so an eye was kept upon her. Was she a bad mother, browned off with these little things that followed her every step? She did have an inclination to wander, for a duck. My mother said that ducklings should be kept dry. Getting too wet chilled them and often they died. I have no recollection of a duckling ever reaching maturity, eager as I was to find a duck I could claim as my own.

Staying with my cousin Mabel in the crofting township of Skerray, some distance along the coast, I couldn't believe the number of ducks they had. Mabel, older than me by a couple of years could not understand why I wanted to play with these boring creatures.

She was coming back on the bus with me and as we departed, her mother put into my hands a brown leather shopping bag with the head of a Khaki Campbell duck sticking out. It was a lovely duck, long and skinny, and very friendly. I was over the moon, but when we got to the bus stop, we tried to push the head into the bag so nobody could see what we were taking on board. Young as I was, embarrassment among adults came easy to me.

Mabel persuaded the duck to keep its head down, but, bored on the journey it was not long before we had the duck popping its head up, and each time the head poked out of the bag, a loud quack reverberated through the bus, turning heads. We were in back seats and thought it highly funny, but the closer we got to our stop, the less funny it got. We now could not stop the duck loudly protesting its dislike of the journey. We squabbled over who would take the noisy bird off the bus for no way would it keep its head lowered into the bag. It had had enough of us.

'It's your duck, and if you don't take it, I'm leaving it on the bus.' She would have too.

With red faces we trudged from the back, all heads turning to watch, catching a glimpse of the duck as we tried to rush it past the laughing passengers. In those days the bus had a conductor and Davy Henderson was highly amused, but the driver was not! A scolding from him for mucking about had us debating on the mile walk from the Pole, would anyone tell our mothers, but a huge squelchy noise from inside the bag had us giggling again. Ducks really can be very messy creatures.

By the time we got home, the duck was quiet and my mother was delighted with this largesse, using duck eggs for her baking and hoping to have a bit more control over this duck that Sandra's wayward fowl. I quickly presented my new friend to its companion. They got on great, but the muddy pool was more inclined than ever to dry out during a long, hot, summer.

Betty's home, a few hundred yards up the road from ours, had a well in the front garden, all the gardens being large and running on a slight slope towards the road. You had to go up a flight of steep steps to get into their front green but this proved no problem to our wandering duck. Their well was deep with steep sides and it was into this death trap Sandra's duck went, seeking water for a swim one particularly hot day. The discovery was made too late to save her. We were heartbroken, but people didn't take much heed of weepy children who spent their summers either on holiday in Scullomie, or Skerray, or running wild on the hills of Kirtomy.

Whatever else, we were used to good food, and particularly so on a Sunday when we sat down with our father, home for his short break from the weekly hard life to catch white fish in the wild waters of the North Sea. My mother knew her meats and the traditional Sunday joint was one to be savoured.

The soup was usually Scotch Broth, and the meat carved by her at the table. We didn't know then it was the domain of the male of the species, to carve the joint. Ours was not a divided household asserting whose right it was to rule the roost…or the roast!

That hot Sunday, we started to eat the main course, delighted we were having a hen for a change. Fowl was not a meat carried by the butcher's vans that served the village and one of our hens had to prove itself useless before it landed on the table. At times one errant bird was plucked, drawn and trussed up to head south to Glasgow or Edinburgh where aunts made short work of this delicacy from their homeland, especially during those hard years of rationing after the war.

I still recall racing in from school, the pungent smell of singing accosting our nostrils as we rushed in the door. Our mother, in the scullery, holding a naked bird over the primus stove singing away the last of the down after plucking its feathers, kept a special task for us. The bird always looked grotesque, with its long yellow claws and feathered head still upon its neck. Why it remained in that condition before its travels, I do not know, yet, it was the way we saw fowl hung when birds became more available, not like today, all tucked in and rounded with no reminders that it was once a living creature with glossy rich coloured head feathers, and healthy strong yellow feet for scraping. Why? Just glimpse into a battery farm and you'll get your answer. And of course, the inevitable health and safety rules. I wonder why we were all so very healthy then.

Crowding round the spluttering primus with its blue flames, we were told, 'Go, the pair of you, and start wrapping the eggs on the table.'

There we found a heavy cardboard box, with large black writing on the lid, 'Eggs With Care' It was sectioned into 12 compartments, each with a corrugated cardboard wrap, waiting for the big, brown, egg we so carefully wrapped in strips of newspaper we first cut, then warily fitted each precious egg into the box. Along with the hen, this would arrive safely, that known when a newsy letter of thanks arrived by return. There was no phone then, nor was there a TV so plenty of time to write interesting letters.

Rationing affected us all, and at school Sandra and I drooled over the sweets some of the children were able to buy at the shop we all raced to during the intervals, whether or not we had money to spend. It was run by two elderly ladies, and we blithely told Forbie that our mother said we could buy on tick. Forbie never checked, and when found out, our mother's wrath was more about the coupons she had to forfeit to cover our stealth than the cost of the sweeties we had seen go into the big ledger taken from behind the counter. We were firmly dealt with and Forbie got a bit of a flea in the ear too.

As we ate that Sunday, Sandra smiled over her plate. 'This hen is really good.'

Without a beat, my father, who became well known in the family for putting his honest foot in things, laughed. 'Lassie. That's not a hen, it's the duck.' Our mother's hard kick connected too late to avoid the inevitable.

'What duck?' Sandra and I gasped together.

'The dead duck, the dead duck, we're eating the duck,' Muriel chorused, not giving a hoot. Still to start school, she knew best what went on in the house in our absence.

We were offered the fall-back for all who moaned they could not eat any particular dish: tatties and milk, but we refused to eat anything in protest. Not even the trifle that was an art in itself and always served up on a Sunday, along with jellies and soft tinned fruits.

The moral of that story is, would you, who had learned during hard times never to waste food, have put the duck on the table, or had a family burial with two little girls as chief mourners? Or would you have lied and said, 'Yes, it's a good hen, isn't it!'

Maybe that's why I had to expunge the memory of grief associated with ducks and change it to hilarity. My Khaki Campbell lived to a good old age, but I never forgot the drowned duck.

The Highlands & Islands Development Board had a bit of a reputation for funding some ridiculous schemes during its lifetime. About the time it metamorphosed into the new Local Enterprise Companies, in 1991, I ran seminars for the HIDB developing the need to see bed and breakfast operators as business people who had as many rights as others to the financial assistance that would see the B&B industry become a vital sector of our economy. I was, therefore, well aware of some of the anomalies within the system.

On a girls' night out in Melvich Hotel, the subject came up.

'How is it some people get whatever they want, and others get nothing, no matter how good their plan is?' Whoever could answer that had the key to riches, and it wasn't me, but a fun-filled conversation on what could and could not get grant aid threw out a challenge to put in a 'spook' application, to see if the new LEC, despite being run by the same HIDB personnel, would view things differently.

Of course, the brief went to my head and the following application was posted, under the guise of a Delilah Mackay, the pseudo name I used when helping set up a local newspaper and fancied my chances as an Astrologer writing humorous Horoscopes. That was fun because one could find out the birthdays of some of the people who got up to no good, and astound, as well as terrify, them with the accuracy of my predictions.

The application was dated 1st April, an ominous day for such a prestigious company to make its debut into our community. All the companies mentioned in the application existed in Caithness & Sutherland at that time, some doing a great job, others doing exactly what, one often wondered. The business plan was headed: Duck Viewing Observation Centre, and keeping to the criterion of diversification, it started:

Are you the right people to tell me how to get myself diversified? I have this croft doing nothing, and this man doing less so money is scarce and its awful galling to be reading about all the money you're desperate to pour out to them that can diversify, so long as they come up with a plausible idea. I have this grand notion to expand my two ducks. It will take a lot of money and her at the back said, just you go to the HIDB if you want money. They have plenty. Now they've disappeared into thin air with all that money, but I heard they left you at the LEC with a big legacy. Wasn't that magnanimous of them in this day and age of grab and take.

Now, do you know about ducks? I made a lifetime study of them myself, as a hobby of course, there being little

139

else to do in this remote parts other than idly observe how the beasts go about it. That is, until I began to study how the HIDB, the NSCSS, NOSCAD, the CCs, HIE, ATS, RES, NCC, SSSI, NIREX, ESAN, CEC, STB, the WRI and the Wee Frees go about it. This now takes up all of my time but there's no money in it.

What I have in mind is this Observation Centre, maybe on the lines of the Post Office Tower but not so elaborate. Why ducks you may well ask? Well, I did think of goats, but you have to be upwind of them and as the wind is in a perpetual circle out here, I have to rule out the goats. As for sheep, did you know a ram does it five times, in quick succession, to the same ewe before he is satisfied he did it properly. I thought that was too much wear and tear on the merchandise for most ewes egg him on. And I'm in this for a profit.

Then, there's this sudden notion for llamas, but what if they showed dissatisfaction with the occasional poor service and spit in the eye of the paying public? Yon permanent look of 'is that it' on their faces would put any suitor off. I could rely on the rabbit, but sometimes you can get too much of a good thing.

Now heifers are very willing participants, but there's an awful nonchalance in the way they take it all for granted and that's no use for my purposes of entertainment. I blame the AI man myself. How any decent man can make his living from such outlandish behaviour, I don't know. Mind you, at the other end of the spectrum, you have the horse! Always ready to perform to the gallery, a natural show off, forever comparing, 'I'm bigger than you!' 'Yea, but mine is bigger than yours!' But there's too many times they expect human assistance and that's no use at all. What if I were left on my own to hold the fort, without a man, and the fellow I have here is useless. Well, maybe not entirely useless! But I can tell you, it's not the holding of the fort that would worry me. It's no job for a woman, that.

No. You just won't get a better performer, for intuitive anticipation, eager motivation, excitable participation and job satisfaction, than the duck...

The application goes on, identifying the educational aspects and the value to the community, and do you know what? The LEC asked an officer to call at the address – an empty house in Kirtomy. They just could not be certain whether they were dealing with an eccentric or was someone taking the Micky. They proved they had a sense of humour when they allowed the letter to be published in a local paper.

As time moved on, I was invited to take a seat on their board. I never ever let on I had any dealings with a certain Delilah Mackay!

Chapter 15

*'Horse sense is the thing a horse has which keeps it
from betting on people'*

W. C. Fields

Horse Sense

Ownership of a horse had never entered my wildest dreams, and one thing for sure, this was not an animal to land with by default! From the moment he could talk, our son wanted a horse. Not a pony. That was not a familiar term, there being no such animal round about us, nor did any of our family or the friends we had then own an equine of any kind. Difficult to imagine today with every other person sporting a pony or a horse in a field nearby.

The child convinced the father and in time Himself came up with the goods. Nobody told us you shouldn't give a nine month old foal to a four year old child who expects to be romping about on its back next day. Nobody said, don't take a spirited Arab for a small boy's first pony, whatever else you do. Nobody said, you need to know a lot about horses before you even think about getting one. But I'm glad they didn't because we knew nothing about keeping a horse, and ended up with exactly what we shouldn't have got: a nine-month old, part-Arab, chestnut foal who had newly returned with his mother after taking the out and out championship at the Mini-Highland show on the Black Isle, having first won the foal at foot sector. He was beautiful, which was a bonus, and he was kind, which was a blessing, because the deal was done before I laid eyes on him. Nobody said, for goodness sakes, see the animal first. I was put right on everything, after we got the animal.

'We've been told we should have got you a donkey first, Neil.' I got a withering look.

'And you were going to call me after a bear too!' was his response. His paternal grandfather had been called Rupert and I liked the name, but thinking there would be lots of opportunities to use it, I started off with naming him after my two brothers and father.

The foal's owners were inordinately proud of him, having two breeding mares in their stable in Caithness along with this foal, and his older brother, as well as a foal belonging to the other mare. We brought home Trouba D'Or, his Arab Society registered name, called him Troubie, although the little girl next door told her mother he was called Droopy Drawers! We got him at a good price because of the caveat, 'For the next season, you'll show that fellow. He's a topper and you'll win with him. Show him under our stable and I'll put a luck penny in your hand,' she told Neil, and she did. The other essential was a good home. That was always the first priority for Alice and John. How we qualified I'll never know. But neither party regretted it over our long association involving horses.

'Sure we will,' I said, smiling at Neil's glowing face, never for one moment knowing what I was letting myself in for. It seemed another good idea at the time. The Greens knew their horses, were past masters in the art of showing and I was lectured to within an inch of my life. The ensuing cost was not even considered, which proves my ignorance. That inescapable fact became a great incentive to drive on with the B&B to finance this new venture that took over a large part of our lives. The pot was divided between ploughing back into the business – I had to fulfil my vision of what a B&B should be – and supporting the horses.

From the day he attended his first show, Neil pushed me to attend the next one. At four in the morning, after returning late the night before, I just had to touch him, and the four-year old child sprang out of bed. Not so smart in later mornings when it came to school though! He lost the art completely by the time he reached teenage years, and on leave from the Marines, it took a sergeant major bellow to have effect. But this was different so off he would go in the cab with the driver, and I would catch up later once I'd bribed my sister Sandra or our cousin, Hazel, to do the rest of my work for the day. The one thing none would do for me was cook breakfast so I didn't escape Scott free, but the minute the last dish was served, I was out that door with the Guest House a million miles from my mind.

Shortly after Troubie joined us, we realised the pony was lonely, despite the sheep we now ran on the croft being happy to befriend him. We also made the mistake of asking Alice when could Neil back the pony.

You'd think I offered to take the pony out and shoot it. 'What! You'll no put a weight on that chiel's back until he's well over two years old. Don't even think about it.'

Nobody had said, you wait at least two years before backing a fine-legged animal like Troubie. Nor had anybody said, the horse is a herd animal, you can't expect one to be happy on its own. They like to have a mate to talk to, to boss about, to share things with or to fall out with. We had a lot to learn and my first hard lesson was the arrival of a borrowed miniature Shetland stallion, to keep our leggy colt happy, and to seriously boss him about, despite being half Troubie's size. As far as Pixy was concerned, size didn't matter. Nor did genus, though gender must have. He never once tried to jump on Himself's back but eyed me with interest each time I came near him. Neil was quite indignant when his pals insisted Pixy was his pony and Troubie its mother! As said, at that time the children were not familiar with horses of any type, but they soon cottoned on, diminishing any popularity I may have had with their parents.

In time, the girls who flocked to our home after the animals arrived all pestered for, and got, sensible Shetland

144

ponies of their own and Neil looked so funny riding out on the 14hh Troubie with the girls on their Thelwells. They all became good friends, the dedicated gravitating towards bigger ponies of their own, and coming to many of the shows with us. A number of years later, a B&B in the village started a trekking centre, so from no equines at all, suddenly we had a village that rang to the sound of hooves hitting tarmac as a string of ponies went about their business.

Pixy belonged to Alice and John, was a little monster and played them up like the spoiled brat he was. If you dared turn your back on him, his hooves were wrapped round your ears when he tried to mount you. He did nothing he was told and much though Alice wanted to show him under saddle, no way did he allow it. Thrown into the deep end of showing with such a lot to learn, it was good that Neil took to it like a duck to water, taught to ride by Mary on Troubie's mother, Tosca. We were entering into a busy and exciting phase and I embraced it with total enthusiasm. The Woman magazine was dumped for The Horse & Pony and stopping up late to see the end of show jumping on TV had us bleary eyed in the mornings. Himself thought we were mad.

Memories are still strong, bringing back smiles at the oddest of times. Neil was very young, maybe five, always independent, taking off to suss out the show field the minute we arrived. Many a time, in desperation, I had to send a message to the show tent and ask the organisers to tannoy him to get back in time for his event.

One day I headed off to find him, and Alice went to get the event tickets leaving the horses tied up to the side of the horse box. We returned to find Neil curled up at the side of the lorry, sound asleep in a bed of hay. Tosca was standing over him, looking about her anxiously, whinnying softly as she saw us approach, as if to say, how could you leave your foal unattended. It's hard to believe that at the age of 14 Neil became allergic to hay and horses, completely destroying any hope of moving from Troubie to the horse I got to complete our stable and ensure his pony would never again feel lonely.

Pixy, on temporary loan from Alice and John's stable, played us up. Troubie played us up, taking his lead from Pixy, and the bigger he got, the worse he behaved. The following summer Neil started school and I met a much wider set of parents once I got involved in the school curriculum. I met and became friends with the Jardines who ran a holding several miles away and happened to own Troubie's half-brother, Maeshowe, out of the same stallion, Ashby Pica D'Or, known as a great jumper before going out to stud. Janet Jardine taught me the rudiments of horsemanship that allowed me have some authority over my errant equines. Janet eventually started a hacking centre of her own on her father's land, fitting well with her mother's foray into B&B, but initially it was just Maeshowe and then her horse, Behan, slowly building to a string of very fine animals, giving us no end of pleasure, and pain, as the years rolled on.

Troubie was always spirited but I wanted to keep him as long as possible before gelding. Two years down the line, at one county show, with the pony big enough to be really strong, a call came over the loud speaker for the owner of the chestnut in Cormack's box to get back there as he'd leapt over the gates and was kicking up hell. I could hear his high pitched hysterical neighing long before I saw him. He was OK – we'd only been gone minutes – but how he achieved this feat in such a confined space stunned us all, leaving the driver shaking his head. He was showing signs of a very spirited temperament. I spent the rest of the show trying to control him as he foamed at the mouth and screamed after every mare he sniffed on the air, throwing himself down on the ground, rolling about like a demon, then rising to his feet to rear up at nothing at all. It was a complete nightmare, isolated to a quiet corner of the huge show field struggling with a hyper pony. I immediately booked him in at the vet's. By now McGregor's had the first of a number of new vets that helped the practice grow to what it is today.

This young man arrived to geld the pony, preferring to do it in the park, that being more hygienic than a stable, he said. Then I was told to get a good grip on Troubie's head collar while he administered the anaesthetic. 'He can go down any second so get ready to stand back. Then get down and hold his head.'

'Me?' I looked at him aghast.

I had slipped on boots to catch the pony for him but I was dressed to welcome guests, not to operate on horses. This was not my scene. Aaah! The thought of all the blood, and knives, and an array of torturous looking instruments twinkling in the sunlight left me weak at the knees. This was above my pay scale, for sure.

The vet looked about him and said, 'There's no one else that I can see.'

So the deed was done and when I told Janet, she looked at me with such envy. 'Oh, I wish it had been me. I would love to have helped with that.'

We were in ways like chalk and cheese, but I liked her immensely and we had years of fun with horses, although it was with her mother, Barbara, I had a particular friendship, one of the cleverest people I'd ever met, and one of the most prone to disaster, landing in situations you couldn't dream up. The horses loved going up there and their horses loved coming down here, so it was a mutually rewarding relationship. Without their encouragement, I would never have enjoyed horses half as much as I did. Nor got into half as many scrapes, especially with Barbara, who had a wonderful aptitude for turning an ordinary outing into a fiasco. But she sure knew how to put food on the table and would go to the ends of the earth to help her family, or the downtrodden. The fact she did not consider me to be one of the downtrodden was at the root of the very few spats we had, otherwise I never laughed so much in all my life as when sallying forth on an outing with her. My age lay slap in between her and her daughter's, so it could be tricky at times, but always worth being out with either of them. However, you had to grit your teeth and close your eyes if Barbara was at the wheel. Just recently Sandra arrived a bit late for a meeting and was immediately offered a cup of coffee. 'I think a Brandy would suit me better,' she gasped out, plonking down into a seat. 'We take it you got here with Barbara, then,' was the only response!

Janet owned this part Irish Clydesdale called Behan, teaching me to ride on him, and Heather, the youngest daughter had Maeshowe, though I preferred Behan. The two half-brothers had a very on/off relationship, either best buddies or rearing at each other or chasing to try and bite each other's bums, then not talking for ages, but both always gave Behan his place as lead horse.

In time I evented with my own horse, Bronco, and whilst still learning the art of jumping, Barbara and I went to a cross-country as jump judges whilst Janet and Behan evented. It was known for being a very tricky course. I was put to judge a water jump and Barbara the large shallow depression dug out like a coffin, last obstacle before the gallop home. It was an evil day of driving sleet, wind and rain, with a big field of competitors. I was numb with cold by the time Janet, the last rider out easily cleared the water jump, yelling, 'Fantastic!' or words of similar triumph as she sped on. It was one of the first jumps and she had a long way to go, but I was able to leave my post and quickly cut across to the coffin and snuggle down beside a desperate looking Barbara.

'I'm frozen to the marrow, and if I don't get to a loo this instant, I'll die.'

'Me too. This is agony. There's no loo unless you walk half a mile to the horse box.' We were snookered. The rain was still driving in, and once you start talking about a pee, well there's no holding back. Until then, I'd coped. Now I was jumping up and down like a two year old causing a scene in the supermarket.

We looked out across the fields and Janet had a good number of jumps yet. The penultimate rider came charging up to the coffin, an easy jump in and out again, shouting, 'Oh, I got a couple wrong,' before tearing off for home. 'I don't think there's been a clear round yet.' I shouted over the wind.

'None of them have faulted here,' Barbara said, straightening up. 'Oh, god! Listen, I've got to go, I can't wait another minute,' She jumped into the shelter of the coffin, not that deep, more of a step down and out the other side for the horse, but with one pee leading to another, I rushed in after her and back out before Behan came thundering up, Janet euphoric, shouting, 'He's going great! A clear round!'

She was very competitive and had this one in the bag - the coffin was a walkover for Behan. The words were barely out of her mouth when, bang! Behan stopped dead. How she kept her seat, I don't know. Behan's head went down into the coffin, as she struggled to push him on, but no way was he stepping in there. I think it was still steaming but she may have thought it was a flurry of snow. Then his head went up and he sniffed the air. A swift step backwards and she could have a fault! Oh, hell, I thought, hand to mouth, willing him into the coffin. I felt like kicking his backside.

Barbara and I looked at each other. It was still raining hard, but...her guess was as good as mine as to why he stopped. 'For god's sakes, Behan, get on with it,' we chorused while Janet kept repeating, 'Why?', along with a few other choice words, urging him on, but under no circumstances was this capable horse putting a hoof in there. She had to skirt him round it and head for the finish in disgust.

It was only last year, when visiting here at Stoneybraes, I thought it safe to tell her why!

Chapter 16

'Excitement was plentiful during my two year service as a Pony Express rider.'

Buffalo Bill

One Trick Pony

With Janet able to teach me how to pleat mains and tails, and when possible come to shows with us, we picked up a lot of rosettes for Troubie, and best of all, had a great deal of fun. Such was the character of both Alice and John, there was never a dull moment, snippets coming back to mind like the day I was occupied and suddenly noticed one of the village girls who came to the shows with us was about to lift a mug of coffee to her lips.

'Where did you get that?' I rudely demanded, dropping the brush I was sprucing up Troubie with.

'Your basket,' the girl answered. 'It's so cold, I needed a warm up.'

She'd get more than a warm up if she drank that so I grabbed the flask top from her indignant hands, handed it to Alice and said, 'You need coffee, Alice,' pulling another flask from the basket and pouring coffee for the astonished girl. 'This is much nicer coffee. You take that. Alice will drink any old rubbish!'

'Bloody cheek,' Alice niggled until her nose picked up the waft of brandy coming from the hot coffee and a smile of pure rapture spread across her face.

'You're getting a head start on the rest of us Alice,' I teased, grinning at Janet. You could never be too careful with the children who loved to come to the shows with us but giving them strong alcohol was not on our agenda. Mind you, we did take one young lady back home, desperately trying to remove traces of having spent more time in the beer tent than on her horse's back, her horse cadging a lift with ours when it dawned, most of the field had left without her. We called for a meal at a posh hotel on the way home and when Alice and I returned from ordering up bar meals, there was the honourable lady, booted feet neatly crossed over on the coffee table, sound asleep in a big leather chair, the combined smell of horse and beer gently wafting over the genteel clientele, enjoying their pre-dinner sherries in the resident's lounge!

We did, however, allow the youngsters stand in the horse float with their mounts, illegal I know, but the horses travelled better that way, the riders chuffed to be in with them, and it was a practice Alice carried out before I joined her so I had no say in the matter. I could have stopped Neil doing likewise, or 'my' girls, but I didn't and one day I caught up on the float, pulled to a stop in Brora. Janet had left with the children and horses and now came out of the grocery shop loaded with bottles of drinks and food.

She started shoving the goodies through the stock sides of the lorry where eager hands grabbed them. Every horse on that float could drink out of a bottle, including the young Troubie because that's what they did when travelling. The riders would take a drink then offer the bottle to their ponies who had no trouble glugging it down.

Alice, sitting in the front seat beside me, began to mutter under her breath. The lorry drove off and the riders, realising we were following, all started to shove arms through the slatted sides, waving with an abandon that caused oncoming drivers to slow down and turn their heads. Adding to the spectacle were many flowing tails as the horses backed up close to the opposite side of a lorry used for transportation of cattle and sheep as much as for horses.

'Have they taken leave of their senses?' Alice growled at me. 'If the police see them, we'll be arrested.' For a while we followed the flowing tails and waving hands before they settled to enjoy sharing their breakfast with their four-legged charges.

Things have got a lot more up market since those days when Janet got her hands on the oldest land rover you ever imagined to haul her horse box while we evented together without Alice or the children's ponies. It was a case of a wing and a prayer as we approached any hill.

'Oh,buggar! Stop! Stop! Oh, no, they're not stopping!'

She'd curse the approaching driver as an oncoming car on the single track road did not stop, meaning we had to pull in to the passing place, her desperately trying not to stop. The brake never quite held the weight of the box when both horses were on board. It was heart-stopping stuff, wondering how far it would roll backwards before getting it into gear and grinding forward again, eyes glued to the road in front as if our determined reaching forward could propel the vehicle up the hill. Having her HGV licence helped, but each time we thought that was the end of us and the horses, we vowed it would be the last time. It never was.

Another time we were unloading the full lorry in Dunrobin Castle grounds at a horse show hosted by the Sutherland Constabulary. I handed the prancing Troubie's leadrein to a uniformed policeman, 'Keep an eye on him a minute. He's so excitable.'

Alice grabbed the lead from the copper and handed it back to me, hissing, 'Listen, are you taking the piss? You don't ask the bobbies to act as your groom.'

'Oh,' I said, perplexed at such a blatant faux pas. 'Sorry,' then in defence muttered, 'He's my brother. I forgot he's a policeman.'

She snatched the lead back from me, handed it to Magnus and said, 'Hold that pony. You're as well doing something useful while you're hanging about here.' That was the same day Magnus's boss made his appearance in his full finery. He was taken with the horses and thought he'd like a shot on one. Bronco was chosen as the Inspector was a fairly large man, and prone to a glass of something warming as he did his welcoming rounds, regardless of the uniform he wore. None of us made any attempt to correct him when he did the classic mounting error, ending up looking at the horse's rear end while I doubled up with laughter. Magnus said I did it deliberately. It wouldn't have been near so funny if I had. That was a man who rose to great heights within the Force without climbing on another horse!

As for Pixy, one memorable morning, losing the head completely, I castigated the errant beast as I tried to prepare him for a show. 'What's wrong with you? You are the biggest pain in my life. You don't get it, do you, you little monster!

He was hell bent on getting on my back while making certain nobody got on his. That was it! I had it with him. I tied him to a stout pole behind Fairview, and scrubbed him within an inch of his life, then warned him, 'If you don't stand there and get rinsed in a decent manner, same as Troubie, I'll do it my way. And you won't like it!'He lashed out as I tried to be reasonable, so I did it my way.

It was an incident waiting to happen. It was hard work because we had no water pipe close to the electricity pole, the strongest stanchion around. In years to come, Smudge would frighten the life out of me by making many valiant attempts to get to the top of that tall pole. By the grace of God she never quite made it before suddenly abandoning such frolics.

With annoyance fuelling my determination, I gathered several buckets of water from the outside tap at The Sheiling, and let Pixy have them, full pelt. He was quite stunned. He walked away from his bath, on the lead, boxed up perfectly to go to Alice's with Troubie to join the full complement travelling next day to the show. He surprised his owner by winning a prize for his tiny rider who was so proud of the way Pixy behaved. Mary was astounded as she led him in the ring. I never told Alice what I did. She would have had no hesitation in chucking buckets of water over me.

The winter approached and Pixy went home to Caithness, Troubie relieved as Pixy's back hooves found their target once too often for friendship to develop, me ridiculously happy to see the back of him, Alice and John ecstatic to get the little hooligan back, minding his manners for the first time in his life. The stable Himself prepared was now ready, two loose boxes and a bit of room to stack bales of hay. Troubie was born in a stable and loved his accommodation, but was a mucky pup, his droppings all over the place each morning in this warm building renovated from an old byre, thick stone walls giving an enviable cosiness, and a spare loose box for any pal who wanted a stop-over. What more could a young colt want! But we knew he needed a companion, and I grew desperate to get a horse of my own as time went by and I battled to keep the business running while Himself had no option but to work away from home spending longer in Shetland than he did with us.

I was looking after sheep, with Jock and Glen's able help, Himself leaving home to find work from the moment he finished building The Sheiling, never telling me that at the end of the build, though not in debt, he didn't have a spare penny to call his own, so needs must, and like so many others from the area, if you wanted to work, you had to give up home comforts. Mind you, for many, more craic was found in a working caravan than ever was found at home, and from some of the stories I heard, Himself had his moments, memories to amuse and recall in the comfort of the Stoneybraes dining room when friends call, and I think, good job I didn't know that then!

With our bed and breakfast closed for winter months, and the ram, known always as the tup, doing his duty in the fields, I was tasked with keeping an eye on him. I thought the watching brief was to ensure this pricey gentleman, hired like a gigolo for the occasion, may come to no harm. I never thought it was to ensure he knew which end of a ewe was which, and what to do with the end that should interest him. He frightened the living daylights out of me, squaring his shoulders, dropping his head, and charging! He was bigger than Pixy and far scarier.

I kept well out of his way after that, telling Himself, 'Yea, yea, he's the man, at it all the time.'

He must have been too, but I never saw him doing other than sniffing the wind, his nose in the air and tongue tasting the atmosphere, alarming it itself without threatening me should I dare put a tentative foot into *his* field. Yet the following spring proved his worth as I raced about trying to cope with his new-born progeny and their unpredictable mothers, look after our child, deal with guests, a pony in the stable, and last year's lambs too young and innocent to enjoy his attentions, to feed and keep separate from the lambing flock. I had to look after the dog, a cat and a rabbit all demanding attention, not to mention feeding the birds, a bold blackbird keeping me in my place should I dare to forget them.

Himself, who had never approved my decision to take scary people into the sanctuary of his home, and worse still, take money off them for the privilege, kept well out of their way in his short sojourns home. The guests believed him much too busy on the croft to idle time away with them. Actually, as the years rolled by and people came back annually, never setting eyes on this husband, they looked at the policeman's cap Magnus left on the hat stand in the hall and smiled, convinced the husband was a figment of my imagination and the hat served as a warning to watch your step.

The guests were right about Himself having plenty to do on the croft, but he was a diligent provider, and highly skilled in the building trade, so whenever I told him we really needed better facilities he set to and brought this about. It was great! In no time, the second season after opening in 1968, I had hot and cold in the bedrooms, then a rare luxury in a rural B&B. It put me ahead of the many beds offered locally in spare rooms that were comfortable, hospitable, with generous helpings of good food. However, younger Europeans in particular, wanted more and I could provide it.

Then it was central heating. After that it was double glazing. And a shower, unknown in our village B&Bs at the time with some places either charging extra for a bath or hiding the plug! Informed guests carried their own bath plug! Imagine that! I discovered this peculiarity when a visitor enthused, seeing our plug neatly sitting between the bath taps, 'Oh, you leave the plug.'

'Yes, the plug looks nicer sitting there than twisted round a tap,' I responded, not realising her meaning until she explained and I was able to assure them that yes, they could have a bath, and no, there was no extra charge!

Because we didn't stoop to such practices, I was privy to tales that left me open mouthed in wonder but with enough sense to keep my mouth shut as such standards were not what certain people wanted to be known for! What a long way this was from the standard of hospitality I wanted to offer. So, with a softly, softly, catchee monkey, attitude, we made each improvement when we could afford it, keeping ahead of the field, Himself able to do much of the work, except for two skills he would not touch: electrical and plumbing work.

Dondie, a local electrician, and a gentleman to his toes, did our earlier electrical work. He was the brother of Ronnie who helped save Bendy's life, twin to Lal who married our friend David O'Brien, starting up O'Brien Construction, today one of the finest building firms in our area. Their daughter Jackie O'Brien who came to many a show with us, can be frequently seen on BBC Scotland, reporting her news items in one of the clearest voices in the media.

Our plumber too was highly skilled, capable of crawling through the intricacies of our slowly growing business, supplying the need for a maze of piping in the loft and under the floorboards, to serve the burgeoning facilities. One day I picked him up at his home and from the moment I saw him, he was not in the best of form. He was a great piper, suffering now from the effects of a big celebration with the band the night before. He'd not been in bed. I suspected he was still inebriated but he insisted upon honouring his commitment and got into the passenger seat, silent as the grave. I recognised the pain so did not torment him with chatter.

He was putting hot and cold into bedrooms Himself had fitted into the large loft space, rooms Neil and I were inordinately excited about, knowing they would be ours, and ours alone. That was until Neil hit an entrepreneurial phase and let his bedroom, behind my back.

Sympathetic to Jimmy's hangover, I brought him a tray of strong coffee and some food, but he was so far gone in his misery he never heard me coming up the stairs. Jimmy was a real gentleman who would never in his life pass a rude comment on anything. He was extraordinarily quiet by nature, with a shy smile and kindly ways.

I was about to announce my presence when I heard him mutter, 'Rubbish. Bloody rubbish. Where did she get this trash from? And I'm supposed to do something with this!'

There he was, sitting cross legged on the floor, like a little gnome. Between his knees were the taps I had considered state of the art. They were different, chunky, and shiny, and like a magpie, I was drawn to their allure. I didn't have a clue. When Himself came home and saw them, he condemned them completely. It was only when the chrome peeled and the red and blue identification rings I thought so smart disappeared, I confessed Jimmy Findlay's opinion! It was the first of our bigger renovations and I had a lot to learn.

With these extra rooms upstairs, I could let all three downstairs bedrooms for guests and keep my sitting room. That was vital, allowing the guests to have the big front lounge all to themselves. One of the rooms was a family room which meant we could have up to eight visitors some nights, and it was essential to provide early evening meals as well as the complimentary home-baking suppers every evening. This attracted a lot of business which meant I was up to my eyes in hard work from morning until night, for many years working alone until a bigger renovation and my growing involvement in outside tourism work meant I had to employ help.

There was a queue for my attention starting with Neil. I was determined I would give him as much of my time as possible, and I had the new pony, the dog who continued his social diary activities, impressing all with his shrewd road sense. Today, with different attitudes, a dog seeing to its own lifestyle would be reported to the authorities along with its owner. Back then, roads were far quieter and people less inclined to demand perfection from neighbours; when there was something to crib about, most people put it to you themselves, and Roxy's conduct appeared to amuse rather than bother. With sheep and lambs in constant need of attention and Bendy who could vanish with wild rabbits for hours on end, and Puss-do befriending the feral cats, life was a whirlwind of activities from early morning until after midnight, sneaking time outside to do a bit of weeding by moonlight, otherwise it would never get done.

But the rabbit that took over our house was not Bendy.

Chapter 17

*'Fowl says it does not want to interfere in mongoose's politics
because it is not a member of mongoose's parliament.'*

Jamaican Saying

The Tale Of The Mongoose

The guests leaving that day were all packed up and
coming back, as many do, asked if I'd stand on the doorstep
with one while the other took a picture. But this time Mr
Parker said, 'You know how you had to keep the mongoose out
of the way because my wife said if she as much as got a
glimpse of it again, she wasn't coming over the door. Well, do
you think you could get him and when Catherine is standing in
the doorway for a picture, hold the mongoose over her head.
She'll never notice. When I show her the photo, she'll have a
heart attack.'

Oh, boy. Was that what he really wanted? But he was
full of fun and I knew what he meant. This was only one of the
many things I was asked to do in the number of years the B&B
continued to flourish from that tentative start, giving Neil as
much of my time as I could, and hold on to the social life we
had in the village, yet ensure the business developed in the way
it should. The dedication paid off, the previous year allowing
us a fantastic holiday in Thailand. That's where we got the
mongoose.

That's not strictly true. *We* didn't get the mongoose.
It was Himself who fell in love with the blessed creature, not
me, but as ever, if he was willing to go along with my ventures
into the unknown, I happily agreed to his, though I didn't really
like the mongoose at all. They have this way with their eyes,

and their teeth are like needles. It could kill cobras, for goodness sakes! He was called Rikki Tikki Tavi – what else!

I should have listened to my instincts. When we arrived at Heathrow with our new-found friend, we were in serious trouble. Waiting for us were Tony and Anne, our friends whom we met when they first stayed at The Sheiling, coming every year since and becoming so close we agreed to stay en route home from holiday. Once over our door, they seemed much more like friends we'd known for years. They came from Ireland and lived in London. They had some wait for us that day!

I suspect I saw a flutter of relief in Anne's eyes when we were eventually released and told her Rikki Tikki Tavi was impounded. Himself had to go home without his impulse buy. The annoying thing was, he is the least likely person I know to act upon a whim, and now we had to endure the attentions of a very irate Customs officer.

HM Customs were so put out at this absolute ignorance of their rules over what could and could not be brought into the country, I thought I would approach the subject with a bit of humour when, safely back home, I filled in the necessary forms for the appropriate licence to take a mongoose into the country. I sent the following response back to Customs with the requisite information before Rikki Tikki Tavi could travel north to Melvich.

Dear Gentlemen of Customs House
I hope this will not fail to help me get my mongoose back, for therein lies a tale, a tale of woe so sad to tell that began in far off Bangkok, and ended with a custom's man – a nasty sort of block!
He pounced upon my laden case as I wandered through the green, then threw the biggest tantrum that I have ever seen. He flapped his arms and grit his teeth and snarled through scarlet face, 'Rules and regulations prohibit that creature in your case.'

*I stared in mounting horror at our furry little beast, he'd
caused such consternation, to say the very least. 'Oh, mercy
me, I didn't know,' I pled to no avail. 'Your ignorance gets
you nowhere,' said my castigating male. 'I'll confiscate your
mongoose, he'll be held in Custom House. 'In quarantine,' I
dared to ask, but my spirits he soon doused as he glared at me
with narrowed eyes and said, 'You watch your step. If you
want to see your pet again, a licence you must get.'*

*So truly chastened, home again, to conservationists you apply,
for a licence for a mongoose, and back came their reply. You
never heard such questions: his sex, his weight, his size? His
place of destination to the colour of his eyes! The conditions
for his transport, his permanent address? Now, why should this
confuse me? I bet you'll never guess. You see, the mongoose in
my case, for which I was rebuffed, was not a living creature but
was truly dead – and stuffed! Yours respectfully, etc.*

PS Appropriate licence now enclosed.

And, in due course, to our great delight, back came this reply
from HM Customs and Excise:

Dear Madam,

*We 'gentlemen' of Custom House, we truly are offended. Many
are of fairer sex, your facts we'd like amended! Of your tale
we're sad to hear, the tale of your mongoose. What can we
say? What can we do? There's really no excuse. The Customs
man, he was quite right, what else was he to do but apprehend
your furry friend and take away from you. In this warehouse
now he sits, a licence he'll await. How long will it be he asks,
what will be his fate?*

*Oh, Mrs Campbell, then you sought a permit for your pet, but
when you put it in the post, the blue you did forget. This copy
must be signed and stamped, and then to you returned, so sorry
Mrs. Campbell but your friend is still interned!*

*He sits and dreams of Highland Tales, here he feels quite lost.
And now we reach another stump, the question of the cost. So
send the blue to us post haste but don't forget the lolly; it's*

three pounds ninety-five for post – a trifle for your folly. When we receive the blue and cash, to you we'll gladly send, a sorrowful little mongoose whose heart we won't offend.

When next you travel, do not err, remember a lesson learnt and then with best intentions, your fingers won't get burnt. Tell your friends and clansmen that tales of woe abound of many a poor wee mongoose that's lost to Customs pound. Yours faithfully, etc.

The blue was duly completed, the cheque written up, and sent with the following and final reply.

Dear Lady of the Custom House

My boob, you have forgiven! Such work to get my mongoose back, that I was sorely striven. And I must say, we all agree, what a super sense of humour. Had I but only known of that, I'd have sent for him much sooner.

I now enclose the money, and the blue that I forgot, though your last communication – more worry it has brought. I see rows of poor wee mongooses, all waiting in a line. When you send one to the Highlands, are you sure it will be mine?

You see, mine was really bonnie, though a leer upon his face, and his left eye it was winking when I put him in my case. For the others, I am sorry, I cannot take them all, but if you come to the Highlands, I hope that you will call. Yours sincerely, etc.

After an assuring telephone call from Customs to say they would never dream of mixing up their mongooses our furry friend arrived and was unboxed to resounding cheers and clinking glasses, the toast being to the ladies and gentlemen of HM Customs and Excise. What sports!

This mongoose sat on The Sheiling vestibule floor, a reasonable talking point, and bothering none until Catherine Parker took exception to it. She wasn't the only one. Smudge, the kitten from hell, gave it a duffing on so many occasions I boxed it up and in a huge gut-out of some really good books, packed it off to the local school, for educational purposes.

Sometimes Smudge would come in and forget to spit at it. She'd actually turn back, give a loud hiss and continue on her way. She could have been spitting at the rearing cobra, Rikki-Tikki-Tavi was in the process of killing. This probably tells you more about Himself than it does Smudge. She was merely following her instincts. What instinct he was following I'll never know.

But Smudge – and her not the size of tuppence, didn't just rid the house of the mongoose. She rid it of all our guests during that first two weeks after taking her from the SSPCA. The straw that broke the camel's back came about that never-to-be-forgotten day when I went into the dining room to pick up the fruit plates before main course breakfast was served.

I could hear Connie going happily about her business, quietly humming an old Irish ballad, having made her point once again, that taking a black and white kitten into our household was just asking for it. They had minds of their own, trouble making, different from other cats. So much had gone wrong in the first week of having Smudge with us, I was beginning to think Connie could be right.

We had a full table and there was an air of hilarity as I walked in. Things had been quiet before when I introduced guests who had not met the previous evening. I smiled, loving the atmosphere created when guests breakfasted in conviviality, picking up on each other's places to go and what they'd all done yesterday. Sometimes unbelievable coincidences took place when similar accents proved one couple lived down the street from another, never having met until staying at The Sheiling! The sun was streaming through the window and I felt we were slowly coping with Smudge's problems. As I picked up plates, ready to contribute to small talk, guests were actually sneaking looks at each other and having a quiet smile. Whatever had been the topic, all talking stopped, yet I detected an expectant hush. This was a bit disconcerting.

My eyes skimmed every surface, but Smudge was nowhere to be seen. Two of the guests had breakfasted yesterday, the others were new. Yesterday I had walked into the dining room to a slightly different atmosphere. Quieter. Not the usual chat. At first I didn't notice, but then someone pointed towards the buffet table. There was Smudge, standing on her hind legs, and dipping a paw into the milk jug, but not looking at what she was doing. Just staring intently at me: I'm such a helpful kitten, I'm entertaining your guests!

'Smudge!' I yelled. She didn't move, but I did, yanking her off the table, out the door and through to the kitchen, milk jug in hand. I thumped the jug down on the worktop. The kitten immediately struggled, offering to scratch so I let her go.

'Connie,' I gasped. 'She had her paw in the milk jug.'

'Milk isn't good for her. Especially with her problems,' Connie answered as if such behaviour was acceptable.

'Connie, she had her paw in the guest's milk, in front of their noses.' She looked at me then, cocked her head to the side and answered, 'You mean, she should be more discreet. Black and white cat, Joan. Told you. No discretion.'

I knew she was teasing me, but she suddenly added, 'And while we're at it, I'll tell you something else. You know the Otters, the ones you drooled over with your nose pressed up to the jeweller's shop for six months, while I wondered if the Devil had got you at the Split Stone, you were so late in coming home. The otters you forfeited a holiday to get and you were advised, for their safety to put a glass dome over them for protection. But of course you didn't. Well, you should have.' I knew this was leading somewhere and Smudge was at the root of it.

'Tell me in a minute when I sort this out,' I answered, heading off with fresh milk. It was a much admired large Border Fine Arts rare edition Connie was talking about. It

164

would not have looked right covered by a dome and had come to no harm in the guest lounge...but its days could be numbered judging by Connie's raised eyebrows while she studied the bright eyed kitten who was watching from a position easily read as: I'm ready for off if you come after me.

'I only wanted to say, next time you know she's about but you can't see her, don't bother looking up the chimney. She'll be perched on that branch in the middle of your expensive ornament, peering out at you, surrounded by otters, and you'll hardly see her, and how she's never broken one of these delicate primroses I'll never know. Caught her there twice now.' The last was delivered in triumph as Connie swung out the door.

'Aahhh!' I spat, just as good as Smudge, for she thought nothing of spitting at you if she was caught in an act of devilry. As I repaired the buffet table after her sojourn up there, full of apologies, replacing the bread waiting to be toasted, the fruit would be renewed each day anyway, it all being fresh and the guests had already helped themselves before Smudge leapt up with the same intent. The prunes and the dish of carefully cooked fresh rhubarb, a speciality of The Sheiling, would not be the first food to hit the dust bin since Smudge arrived. I sighed heavily. What had I let myself in for! Felix had never behaved like this. Oh, Felix had her moments, but slowly her memory was taking on saintly status.

Maybe Smudge was reacting to hearing, 'Felix would never do that,' every other hit. But all that was yesterday, and this was today, and Smudge was nowhere to be seen so whatever was going on in the dining room? It couldn't be down to her, could it?

I quickly left and checked in the mirror. Nothing on my face. I hurried down the corridor and into a bedroom to find Connie. 'Is there anything that shouldn't be there stuck on my back?'

'Why?'

'Never mind why, just tell me.'

'Nothing out of the usual. That I can see,' she added, slowly walking round me. 'Apart from the big hole on the backside of your trousers.'

'What?' I screamed, hands clamping my bum.

'I'm winding you up! That little monkey is making you lose your sense of humour.' But it was not my humour that would be lost to us, something more precious and more costly.

I went back to picking up the rest of the plates, nervous, sure something was amiss. My eyes sped over every visible surface, but no kitten. Nor was she perched in the primroses peeking over the beautifully sculpted mother otter, watching her kits, ready to plunge into the water beneath.

Ken Gordon, who had booked in a couple of days ago, indicated with his head towards the wide window closest to the table. I looked, saw nothing unusual and looked back at him, but he was now looking up above the window panes. We had recently changed the dining room drapes to beautiful cream curtaining with swags and tails. My eye went to where he and everyone else were staring.

And there she was. Only her nose and eyes, positively dancing with devilment, poking out of the folds of material draped across the top of the window, her excitement making her eyes squint even more. She was intently watching everyone. The minute she spotted my open mouthed stare, she spat. She had a way of spitting, screwing up her nose until it wrinkled, her tongue going into the roof of her mouth and the spit came out almost as if she lisped, the mouth pink and wide. From my position beneath her, I saw it clearly. Then she flew. The shock made me see her in slow motion. I can still see it, like a black and white flying squirrel. We probably all gasped as she landed right in the middle of my beautifully set table. There was a collective holding of breath. It's a big table but instead of dashing off towards the side, she shot down the length of it, away from where I was standing, skipping over the bread plates and scooting round the teapots and coffee jugs.

She was gone in a flash and I was left there dumfounded. Nervous laughter filled the silence. Then they looked at me expectantly. What could I say. Five star service at its best! Profuse apologies, eyes on the couple who knew this was not a one off, same kitten had made its impact yesterday in the milk jug and got off with it. After restoring order, grovelling, admitting to being beat by feline behaviour that demanded hide and seek games at least twice a day, and they were quite exhausting, little walks up the hill morning and night. I seriously sought their advice, and those lovely guests were happy to discuss the problem and stayed on to honour their reservations. That didn't stop me from leaving the dining room defeated.

'Connie. Take no more bookings. The minute the house empties, we're closed. I'm closing down. I honestly can't take any more.'

She looked at me in astonishment. 'Never!' It was her favoured response to the incomprehensible.

Nothing ever, in the long years of existence, before Smudge, had come between me and my business, opening on 1st April without fail, closing at the end of October, but in between, every day was worked. I loved the hard reality of delivering dinner, bed and breakfast, to the finest of people, many who stayed for anything up to a month, year in, year out, June being a month that saw so many of the same people, we had the most wonderful house-party atmosphere. And nothing disrupted that until today. The dye was cast. Smudge had to go.

This time Connie sadly shook her head, no teasing humour behind her statement, 'Black and white cat. She can't really help it. It's in her genes.'

Chapter 18

'Don't estimate the value of a badger skin before catching the badger.'

Japanese Saying

Badger For Breakfast Anyone?

As we cleared up the breakfast table, we did what we always did when problems arose. We talked it over. Heart in mouth at the dreadful decision I just made, and with Connie standing quietly by, I picked up the phone and explained my need. Then I asked, 'Do you think her mother will take her back?'

Before Mr Gunn from the animal welfare centre could reply, Connie raised her eyebrows along with her shoulders. 'Would you, if you were her mother?'

'Go away,' I mouthed as I listened anxiously, phone pressed to my ear. I heard the sigh in his voice before he warned, 'It would be very unusual. She's been with you for a couple of weeks now. Can't understand the tummy problems, she was absolutely fine after coming in here.'

'It's not just the tummy problem. She is completely hyper. We've managed to get her to walk on grass and now she goes mental rushing all over the greens like a maniac. I never know where she is.' I caught Connie's face as she picked up Smudge and quietly stroked her. I knew that if I didn't keep her, it was doubtful any other would.

'Bring her in anyway and we'll see what happens,' Mr Gunn reluctantly advised. Connie gave me that look, quizzical, think before you make this decision. 'I know, Connie, I know. Let me take her in this afternoon and see if her tummy settles, if her mother will take her back. Just for a couple of weeks.

Then I can have her home again.' I had no idea how this was going to pan out but something had to be done.

Connie sat in the front seat but Smudge wanted to stay on my knee, wrapped as ever in her towel, staring into my face. Each time I went out in the car, I took her with me. Safer for her and everyone else, so by now she had accompanied Connie home every day, had gone to the local shop as often as necessary, and come into Thurso shopping for fresh ingredients every other day. She loved the car.

She attracted a great deal of attention outside the supermarket as she skipped about the car, her bin firmly tucked between the back and front seats, her bed on the back seat but herself flying round the head rests, faffing about on the parcel shelf and generally attracting attention. She had absolutely no use for any toy bought for her, the exception being a long-legged fox that hung for years by Felix's igloo. Smudge didn't play with it, but would haul it in beside her to sleep with. The fox travelled with her, in a bid to keep down her excitement, but once in the car, she abandoned it. Fox was a sleeping companion, not for exciting expeditions to the shops. Her anticipation knew no ends when I appeared with the shopping. She couldn't wait for her little dish of chopped chicken, the best the delicatessen could supply for fear of upsetting that delicate tummy. You just had to say, 'It's for the kitten. She travels with me and can't see past your produce.' All sorts of little packages went into the goods I legitimately bought for the table.

She was having the time of her life and here was I, heading back to the home with her, making a dubious Connie my accomplice. Anne was back at Uni but she would have been very upset that the kitten's behaviour was uncontrollable. Connie, who often knew more of my son's activities than I, warned, 'I don't think things are going well there, Joan.' Returning Smudge would not be viewed as helpful.

The moment we turned into the Balmore driveway and cut the engine, the barking engulfed us. Smudge froze. I carried her in, convinced her mother would renege the moment she set eyes on her errant daughter.

'That's amazing,' Mr Gunn said, 'They don't usually take to the kittens once away for so long.' Smudge's little mother was delighted to see her, absolutely no problem at all. 'Can you just keep her for a couple of weeks, until I sort out things so she can't get to guest areas of the house. And maybe she'll grow up a bit in that time.'

Smudge's back went up in an arch, every hair seemed to stand on end. She pinned back her ears and spat at her friendly looking mother. Her skinny legs quivered in indignation.

Connie was standing shaking her head behind Mr Gunn's back, mouthing, 'Black and white kitten. Won't work. Told you.'

We never did find out. In a flash, I had a spitting ball of fury to contend with. I was stunned. No way was she accepting this turn in events. The barking dog could only be heard from the kennels when outside, but however we tried, she was not having her mother. 'We could put her in a pen on her own,' Mr Gunn suggested.

'No,' I said, 'She really doesn't want to stay. I'll take her home.' The grin widened on Connie's face but much though I loved Smudge, how were we going to cope. Just as we were leaving, Mr Gunn handed me a couple of large tins of cat food, not what Smudge was used to, low cost, a brand Felix would not have thanked you for. Nevertheless, I opened a tin that night, leaving the expensive kitten food in the fridge. She recognised this food. She tucked in and believe it or not, though still hyper, her tummy problems disappeared, and young though she was, the bin and liner were abandoned, comparative peace restored and I believed we were over the hill.

'What were you feeding the poor wee thing on?' Connie enquired, looking down at Smudge sleeping like a little angel in the special quarters, build for Felix when our new kitchen was installed. This cat quarters were not on the plan. Health and Safety would have a field day at finding a cat igloo with large sleeping cat ensconced in an alcove next to the stove where all the cooking for the guests was carried out. *Heads on Pillows* gives you the full saga of the Builders' Cat, behaviour we were inclined to forget as we promoted Felix to sainthood in comparison with Smudge.

'We can't have the cat sleep in there,' I had implored, knowing the fuss made by Europe that particular year about B&Bs having their pets in the kitchen. The builders immediately purchased a towel rail, set it in the recess beside Felix's bed, and said, 'That's the area where you keep all your trays and oven cloths.' Not according to Felix, who took to her bed in the recess and became very agitated when an inspector happened to call. Whoever sussed out the 'unusual' guest's identity, they rushed to the kitchen and removed the cat's bed. We discovered a hooded cat igloo to be more hygienic and Felix loved hers with Fox guarding its entrance.

So Smudge's outrageous behaviour was my fault then, all this pooing and all this hyper activity, doling out the finest of kitten food when the charming little creature fared better on middle-of-the-road cat food.

'Right then Connie, back to the coal-face. But, as much as is humanly possible, we have to keep Smudge away from the guests.' I never before allowed any of the animals through to the guests. Except of course for Bendy. They loved him. And the minute Felix smelled the coffee, she trotted in to spend the evening in the guest lounge. Do you know, she was so good, she never ever climbed on to their furniture, or knees. Dennis Shrimpton had a recording of her ecstatic purring. It was so loud! As for Rex, the rabbit that came after Bendy, I had him before Smudge, but I think they had the same teacher!'

Connie had pet guinea pigs and was charmed by my stories of the rabbits I had, cocking a snook at the warning from Himself, after Rex's irascible behaviour, 'There'll be no more rabbits in this house.'

However, after the change of food, Smudge was now behaving better, definitely, but in what seemed like no time she refused more of that particular food. As Himself and I sat eating breakfast, her pitiful stare forced me into giving her a little porridge with milk. She relished this breakfast making a real nuisance of herself if not provided, day in, day out, forever. Never hurt her tummy, so breakfast was sorted. It didn't dawn on me then, that the intense stare may have been to make up for the fact she never would meow or purr. She was growing now and up to all sorts of no good, with lots of time spent outside which gave the house a break from her games, the frights given when she sprang out from corners to pounce on you, your scream putting her into a frenzy of delight. Hide and seek was not merely a one-way game when she found you. Oh, no. You then had to find her, turn and turn about. And she sure could hide. If you were patient and had an idea in the house where she went, and stood absolutely still, barely breathing, a little face would appear round the corner, then you had to pounce and shout, 'I see you.' This was the ultimate in high glee, much better than finding her hunkered down into a hidey hole. Many a poor guest came home early in the afternoon to be frightened out of their wits by their host pouncing out and screaming, 'I see you,' into their face. I would curse the carpeting and quiet shoes when doors were all left open to accommodate the sunny summer days, while trying to explain I was playing with a cat. The cat, of course, was nowhere to be seen.

Then at lunch time, a little face would look up at us, her cat food ignored. I remembered all the vegetables I cooked for the Street's terrier dog, Mr MacTavish, when staying for a fortnight, sometimes a month, with two dogs at times. I offered her a little vegetable soup. Gobbled up in the twinkling of an eye, and as we still did dinners for guests, there were vegetables galore on the go, so the pleading at dinner time ended in a little of what we ate, and no tummy problems. By now she was beginning to hunt and augmented her vegetable and oatmeal diet with her own catch. Other meals had to be what we ate and she was very strict about that. She did not like fish though, no way.

Each day as I hurried to run Connie home at midday, usually the end of her working day with me, the call went out, 'Come on then Smudgie,' the kitten racing to the car to sit on Connie's knee. The moment we reached the house, her working collies dashed out to bark their heads off. Smudge hated them, but seemed to take perverse pleasure in setting them into a frenzy of barking by her leaping all over the car seats and into the back window as we turned to drive home. But if I went in to see Connie's mother, Ciss, Smudge lay on the car floor until I came back out. She was no fool, just needy of constant excitement most of her waking hours.

And believe me, though less hyper, she found ways of causing constant excitement! But there was plenty other excitement we could not blame on Smudge at all.

It was my habit to go out for provisions to what Connie called 'the shed', in actuality our large garage that never saw the tread of a tyre in all its long days. Himself kept it stocked as a workshop with no less than two large freezers inside. We bought fresh local meat in large quantities: a whole Caithness pig; we had our own stock of lamb; meats from Bews Butcher, allowing a great choice of quality produce for the table. And when bringing home three varieties of fish such as kipper and smoked haddock for breakfast, fresh haddock for dinner, it was prudent to fast freeze each individual fish and store in special bags to identify contents when rushing in about midnight to take out what was needed in the morning. I did the same with small quantities of Bews sausages, black puddings and haggis, never knowing which order was needed, and no shop next door to dash out to.

One morning as Connie came into the kitchen, I met her with, 'You're not going to believe what happened here last night.'

Her eyes flew to Smudge, who was waiting patiently for her porridge. 'No, not her this time. But when I get my hands on Neil, I'm going to kill him, this time for sure!'

'Neil?' She looked at me aghast. I don't know why, but in her eyes he could do no wrong. Me? I had a more realistic view of his lifestyle. Neil was blessed with good nature, much like his father. When he came out of the Royal Marines, my outrage at infringements I thought beyond the pale, amused rather than influenced him. He had the same driven working ethic as his father and helped me enormously with the animals when at home, and knew well I was only doing a diligent mother's rant when things reached my ears.

'Yes, Neil! I ran out for the breakfast stuff last night, and at first couldn't find a thing I was looking for. Then I spotted the green bag with the butcher's breakfast stuff. Stuck my hand in and nearly had a heart attack. I swear to you, I had to go in and fortify myself before I went back out and looked to see what was in that bag! My heart was thumping like a steam engine!'

I now had her full attention as I turned back to the stove to get on with my cooking. I swung back round to deliver the killer blow. 'A badger! I nearly jumped out of my skin! That's what I put my hand on. A bloody dead badger, Connie. Would you believe that? In my freezer! *A Dead Badger*!'

'Well, yes,' came the perceptive response accompanied by a knowing shrug. 'I suppose it would have been dead. In a deep freeze all day. And it wasn't in the food compartment.'

'Tell me it's not your badger, Connie?' I had trouble taking this in, especially as I had food to cook and a table to attend. I thought she would be astounded. It dawned on me she was in on this. Was my faithful Connie complicit in this heinous act of treachery?

'What would I be doing with a badger in your freezer, now you tell me that?' With a nod of the head, she turned for the door. 'Not so fast, Connie Mackay,' I demanded.

'Right. A dead badger,' I said, all thoughts of attending the dining room postponed. Smudge was still here so that area would be safe and some were just passing the glass door, heading in for breakfast. I had the wit to close the kitchen door before any talk of badgers in freezers reached surprisingly sensitive ears. 'It's food I keep in a freezer. Not dead badgers. And how did it get into my freezer? Please don't tell me Neil killed it.' He went stalking when he got the chance but like so many outdoor people, had a love of wildlife. He wouldn't have deliberately killed a badger. Would he? Badgers were rarely seen; I'd only ever seen one in my whole life. A living badger, that is. And I only glimpsed at this one, one quick look at its white striped face and staring black eyes was enough. I let out a youl fit to waken the dead, rammed the lid down on the freezer and took off.

I ranted on. 'They're protected animals, for god's sakes. Imagine a health inspector finding a badger among the breakfast ingredients…'

She cut me off. 'It was not among the breakfast ingredients. They were safely out of the way in the other freezer. It just happened to be in the same colour bag as the sausages, and I forgot to tell you that we shifted all the smaller bags into the other freezer and just laid the badger out in a strong green bag on top of…other stuff.'

'Well, it's out of there now! Lying on the garage floor, decomposing as we speak. Don't you move until I come back from the dining room. Neil's stamp is all over this. I just know it. I nearly died of fright,' I muttered, determined to get to the bottom of it.

'Right,' she said, all efficiency, 'I'll make you a nice cup of coffee. Then, you cook and I'll serve, and I'll explain.' Connie had worked in the hospitality industry all her life, was highly trained and well used to sorting out irate proprietors with a bee in their bonnet, except in my base, it was a badger in my freezer.

It didn't take much explanation and she knew I needed humouring. I was ages searching for my ingredients last night, wondering when I eventually found everything in the ice cream, bread and baking freezer, was I was losing it, not remembering putting breakfast ingredients in there. If that happened today, I'd think nothing of it, but back then, my memory served me only too well.

'The boys all went to that dance in Tongue on Friday night. And coming back over Apigill, there was a dead badger on the side of the road, killed by a car. Neil took it home.'

'Why? Why would any sane person take home a dead badger? I bet he was in a worse state than the badger?' My mind boggled over the wisdom of this child I had no doubt neglected at times when I shouldn't, and over-indulged to make up for his home being invaded by strangers. 'What if he'd bumped into a guest, sauntering in here with a dead badger in his arms?' I sighed. 'Connie, other fellows take home *girls*!!!' I threw up my arms in despair. 'My son takes home a dead badger!'

'For goodness sakes. Because he wanted to make a sporran out of it. What other reason would there be? You weren't here, so we put it in the freezer until he found a taxidermist. It's as simple as that.'

'It might have been if someone had told me about it.'

'And would you have allowed him put it in the freezer?'

'No. It's as simple as that! I would not!' I responded and made immediate arrangements for the burial of the badger, so far up the hill I could forget about it forever.

Come to think about it, Neil was only two years old when Sandra caught him using a couple of choice words beginning with 'b' within her hearing. 'What's that you just said, Neil?'

'Bill the Badger, I just said Bill the Badger!' Rupert Bear and his badger friend had been a popular bedtime story. And look where that got us!

Chapter 19

'Never mistrust the rabbit who has taken your money. It may return with a carrot.'

Dr Kyaciss Pfiell

The Year Of The Rabbit

Despite episodes like the badger, I'm blessed that I can remember so many happy times, and so much laughter as we worked. Mention a pet rabbit and I see Connie, coming down the hill at the back of The Sheiling, Benjamin BT under an arm, a finger wagging in front of his broad white nose, lecturing him on his errant behaviour, his long red ears pinned back as he looks at her in defiance. Yet he never bit her, or me, and that could not be said of all his encounters with people.

Approaching her, I heard, '…and after this, my lad, you'll not stay out until this time of night, mucking about with that Floosie! There's a fox up that hill, and one day, he'll get you.'

I was conned into taking Benjamin, that being my best excuse! After Rex, there was to be no more rabbits. When you take a rabbit to live with you, give it the freedom and attention you would give a cat, you find a clever, amusing and inventive pet that steals hearts, no matter how set they are against the idea of a rabbit living in the house.

Connie was well aware of the ban on pet rabbits, but after being with us a few years, remembering Bendy in particular as her son Ellis grew up with Neil, she could not resist temptation, arriving one morning with a box.

Grinning broadly she announced, 'Happy Birthday Joan!'

Thanking her profusely for remembering my birthday, I nearly dropped the box when it moved.

'Oh, be careful of her.'

'Her?'

What her? I wondered, suspicion beginning to dawn. It couldn't be, could it? Himself would kill us if it were, but overriding that thought, an inordinate excitement gripped me. I whipped open the lid and looking up at me was a little black face, the image of Bendy, though something finer about this one. So well there should have been. Bendy came from a local breeder, but Connie had sourced this Rex Rabbit from the south and it came, on the train, with a pedigree! There was no point in saying, 'I have nothing for a rabbit, no hutch, nothing.' What did a rabbit need, other than a house to live in and a family to love it. But Rex had been a totally different creature from Bendy, creating havoc with a talent that made you wonder where he came from! Then there was Benjamin, and we certainly had cause to wonder where he came from, and eventually, where he went. What this little creature would bring to our busy household remained to be seen.

When Himself came off the rig I put, *isn't this the best thing that ever happened* look on my face, 'See what Connie gave me for my Birthday,' imbuing the statement with wonder and pride, the rabbit now quietly settling into being a trained house pet. That my darling husband had forgotten my birthday gave me a head start. He wasn't near as put out as I thought, considering all the rotten things Rex had inflicted upon him, putting a lifetime ban on more 'rodents' in the house, broken by the earlier arrival of Benjamin BT.

'I thought Jet would be a nice name for her,' I suggested, eager to get his endorsement of this beautiful creature.

'More like jettison, if I had my way,' and Jettison she became.

179

She was a good rabbit, and with Connie being so protective of her, any naughtiness was dealt with on the quiet. Smudge was coming up on two years old and genuinely liked the rabbit which was a relief as this cat became a formidable hunter, and with the devil always dancing in those bright green eyes, one never could tell what Smudge would get up to. She never in her life mewed nor purred but that face spoke volumes.

But let me first tell you about BT and his adventurous summer holiday as a guest of The Sheiling. The first I heard of him was picking up the phone to hear, 'Joan, you have to do something about this rabbit. He is so lovely, the image of Peter Rabbit.' My sister's animated voice came down the line. I was heading for a big shopping in Inverness and she had a flat there, above a man who kept rabbits, often housing rescue rabbits until they got owners.

What really appealed to Muriel's sense of humour, I suspect, was the circumstances surrounding this rabbit's arrival there. A police car was moving along the main road in the Black Isle when the officers saw a large red and white rabbit skipping along the grass verge at a fare rate. They pulled over and watched for a while as it continued, very sensibly sitting waiting each time a vehicle sped by. The policemen drove slowly towards the rabbit, afraid for its safety, obviously someone's escaped pet. As they approached, the rabbit turned towards the car. They pulled up and a constable got out the passenger side. Before it could be picked up, the rabbit hopped into their car and up on to the vacant front seat as if he knew he was going somewhere. It was a big, big, rabbit and the officer thought he'd just leave it and sat in the back, after seeing its long yellow teeth when it made that guttural spitting noise rabbits are capable of when alarmed.

Now, that was their story and I'm only repeating what I was told, but it was handed down through a couple of tellings before it came to me. And yes, I was pulled in by the story too. There would be an element of truth in it if nothing else!

We had no rabbit, this being before Jettison arrived, and I was genuinely concerned about taking another house rabbit, not just persuading Himself into accepting it, but Rex had caused so much trouble and I had loved him to bits, bereft when he took ill and died, reminding everyone of the depth of sadness felt when Bendy met his inexplicable death. This Peter Rabbit would have to live in a hutch. Neil had left the Marines and was back from a year in Australia, called up as a Reserve when the Gulf War began; thankfully it was over by the time he got back here, and was now an Operator on the oil rigs, getting home every two weeks.

'Neil, Muriel knows of a rabbit she says desperately needs rescuing. Do you think you could make a hutch for it when I'm in Inverness.' He would do it, I was certain.

I was meeting Himself from the airport, and knew I'd have a bit of explaining to do, so grabbed the wicker cat basket and headed off. Little did I know what I was letting myself in for. It was before Smudge and no problem with Felix, that paradox of virtue who was now heading for her 21st birthday. She had been brought up with a rabbit, and despite hunting adult wild rabbits she had a weird passion for baby bunnies, bringing them home alive and hiding them behind doors, behaving in such an excited manner, I soon sussed them out. Guests would stare through the windows in amazement as I rushed down the land or up the hill to restore a tiny bunny to its warren when I should have been cooking their breakfasts as this was always a morning activity for Felix. At other times she would eat her large rabbit, always leaving what I called a pair of rabbit trousers lying on the back steps. I often wondered why the cat ate the rest but left the best part of the rabbit, the meaty back legs…maybe a gift for me? She was a quiet cat and would never boast of such magnanimity.

Anyway, this new rabbit would have to be protected, just in case she may think of turning him into a pair of rabbit trousers.

When I set eyes on the rabbit, I turned to Muriel, astounded. 'He doesn't look one little bit like Peter Rabbit, and I'll swear he bared his teeth at me!'

'He wouldn't do that. He's just smiling at you. He thinks you're taking him home.' She pulled me away from the man who had him and whispered, 'The other rabbits are bad to him, that's why he has to get a home.' I later found out it was he who was bad to the other rabbits!

'Well, he's no Peter Rabbit. He's more like Benjamin.' And, as we all know, once you name an animal, well, that's it! It's yours! Unless you're cute, like Muriel and know of a softie who'll take the animal for you.

When I picked up Himself at the airport, he had a travelling companion who wanted a lift home with us, so little was said about this unexpected acquisition. His friend had arrived on an earlier helicopter and availed himself of some liquid refreshments while waiting, so was in fine good humour by the time he climbed into the back seat beside the rabbit. His first instinct was to open the basket.

'Please don't open the basket. I don't know this rabbit. Better just leave him to settle.'

The basket still had the small hole Bendy had chewed to allow him escape all those years ago. I tried to drive out of the town keeping glancing at the rear view mirror. I could see the man eyeing up the basket.

'Ouch! Christ! That bloody animal bites!'

I would bite too if a stranger poked a finger into my domain in a strange car, with strange voices all around me. After all, my poor rabbit was used to police protection. I defended the rabbit. Himself took the side of his colleague. It was not a good journey home with a vicious, man-eating rabbit nobody in their right senses would want, according to our inebriated passenger. But as far as Himself was concerned, the rabbit had chalked up his first black mark.

The hutch was ready, packed with straw from the stable in cosy sleeping quarters, with a little hay to nibble and fixed to the mesh was the old water bottle Rex had used on the nights he opted to sleep in the red hutch my father built for him. After one night of incarceration Rex made it clear the hutch door was to be permanently left open, proceeding to share his quarters with Puss-do and the tribe of feral cats they all grew up with. That red hutch met its end when Himself, taking home peats, reversed over it, smashing it to pieces. Despite Rex's determination to alienate the man of the house, he was mightily relieved there were no occupants in the hutch at the time.

So Benjamin was deposited into the new hutch. But, inevitably, it wasn't long before he spent more and more time in the house. By then, I was deeply involved in tourism boards and committees so spent a lot of time in the office that led off the kitchen, the door left permanently open, Benjamin favouring a space under my desk to rest. I didn't realise then his attachment to the house and garden area was because he had sore feet.

Benjamin also gravitated towards where Rex had carved out a bed for himself all those years ago, when that black ball of mischief followed me to bed the nights he spent in the house. We had an old double bed with a hessian covering underneath the mattress, something I knew nothing of until one day Rex went missing and I looked under the bed. The hessian bulged almost to the floor and this weight was swinging slowly back and fore, just like a hammock. This was Rex, and that's where he slept most nights. When in the house he was very strict about timings, supper at 9 o'clock, bed usually by 10 o'clock, but if you went to bed and he was in and you did not check to see if he was in his hessian hammock, shutting the bedroom door resulted in it getting a severe walloping from a pair of very strong back feet. This invariably disturbed guests, but Rex didn't care. Many a time we were drifting off to sleep when, Bang! Thud! Wallop! In a sleep-befuddled haze I would shoot out of bed to open the door and the brat would hop in as if he owned the place. However, should any unforeseen noise emanate up from a guest room, Rex was not averse to thumping right back at them. I would hide my face in shame next morning in case the guests thought it was me warning them like the old harridan of yesteryear's boarding houses, to cut out the nocturnal carry-on.

Now we had another incumbent, but this was a modern bed without a hammock and Benjamin lay under it whenever he wanted to, though mostly he slept in my office. That's where he was lying the day a team of Australian clippers finished the job and came in for a meal. Not only had Connie rolled the wool, she now stayed on to help with the meal.

Sitting in the kitchen with Himself, having the customary dram after a job well done, one of the Aussie's spotted Benjamin through the open office door, lying stretched out under my desk.

'You got a rabbit in the house? What a beauty!' His amazed drawl interrupted my stirring of the soup. He headed for the office as I turned my head to warn not to touch the rabbit. 'Hey!' he yelled, 'this bloody rabbit bites.'

For some time to come, if any guests proved tetchy, we'd whisper a warning to each other: 'Hey! This bloody rabbit bites!'

If he was not in a good mood, yes, he could bite, but mostly he didn't and he never bit a guest or a member of the family. He did however, use his teeth in other ways which was not good, and that's how he became known as Benjamin BT.

The first time it happened, I could not understand what was wrong. The phone line went dead. It was the afternoon before an engineer called and traced a break in the cable leading to that particular phone. There were several cables under the desk, leading from the sockets to computer equipment as well as two telephone connections. In those days you needed one line for calls and another for accessing the internet. I was working on a pet project for the local enterprise company involving a good number of clients, the phone and internet connection essential, so being cut off not only affected the B&B, it could badly affect what I was working on, and always with a deadline. I must have trapped and snapped a cable under the metal feet of the desk. How annoying!

A couple of days later, I had no access to the internet. I spent an hour on the phone with BT, my server, trying to suss out why I had no service, until Benjamin came skipping in the door, straight under the other desk and gave the cable a good rattle. It was as if he were saying, this is what's wrong, you stupid woman! So back came the engineer. This time he saw the rabbit and became suspicious. I coiled all the connections up behind the desk, out of Benjamin's reach.

Another break in connection proved the rabbit could actually stretch up and pull the cabling down. Back came the engineer. In fact, he was back so often as Benjamin sussed out phone cables, not cables to any electrical equipment, or lighting, or TV cables, only phone cables, which were now to be found throughout the house.

One day the engineer looked at me in complete exasperation giving his best advice. 'Look, you're going to have to do something serious about this, move the connections up the wall, because I'm convinced that rabbit has shares with BT and he's going to keep the money rolling on in!'

So Benjamin BT he became, and we learned through trial and error how to keep telephone cables safe. How I wish we had been able to keep Benjamin just as safe

Chapter 20

'The fox should not be on the jury at a goose's trial.'

Thomas Fuller

The Fiery Fox

Eventually the name Benjamin was dropped, the general cry going out, 'Have you seen BT anywhere?' One morning Connie asked that question and I did a quick search of the house. We kept a good eye on BT who loved the garden and spent a lot of time idly lying in the sun, often under a plant, seeming to take his ease. We didn't know his age which could be keeping him much quieter than the young rabbits we had before.

We still had a few wild rabbits romping about the back, though not like the past when the braes were pock-marked with the homes of eagerly nibbling creatures, less and less inclined to scatter, getting more and more used to the comings and goings of a busy household that never interfered with their foraging. But they were meat for any eager fox, the occasional one seen close to the perimeter fence. BT was usually in the garden, or in the park at the side of the house, easily seen, and that is where he found himself a girlfriend.

Hares are seldom seen in our fields, the mountain hare occasionally sighted in the hills of Sutherland, but if you hoped to see one of the big brown hares, you had to go to Caithness. One fine summer morning, I looked out the side gate of the garden and loping down the hill came a young hare. I couldn't believe my eyes. It was a small hare, a fine animal, definitely a hare and because of her fine looks we decided it was female. We saw her often as she came down the hill, cut across the park in front of The Sheiling and crossed the main road, on into the fields stretching towards the bent-grass fringing the beach. We were very worried she would get killed but couldn't stop her daily run to the other side of the road.

Then we caught her eyeing up BT. She would stop at the garden gate every morning, waiting. We worried he would follow her and go to the road as she was persistent, coming into the garden when it was particularly quiet, but BT didn't seem in the least interested in her. However, one fine day the scruffiest little rabbit you ever saw in your life arrived in the garden and Benjamin BT was hooked. She was quite ugly, for a rabbit, and there was something disreputable about her so Connie dubbed her, The Floosie. At first it amused us but then he started following her up the hill and this morning Connie asked the inevitable question, 'Have you seen BT anywhere?' She searched up the hill and I did another trawl of the house.

There he was under the bed, and something about him didn't look right. I persuaded him out and noticed that there was a lump on his foot. I also noticed something I'd never seen on any of our rabbits. His claws were long. The vet soon had that fixed and actually removed the lump. He also checked his mouth and said he had to have his teeth clipped. We never needed to clip our rabbits' claws or teeth because they went out all the time and their scampering about on hard ground and gnawing outside prevented growth that can harm pet rabbits. He said BT must have been a hutch rabbit, in the habit of having his feet and teeth seen to. So long as I knew, I didn't mind the trips to the vet, but I wondered if this was why he was flung out as none in the area he was found laid claim to him.

BT was laid up for a few days, and the hare kept appearing – so did The Floosie! 'She's nothing but a Tart. Trying to entice our BT when he should be going about with that lovely hare,' Connie insisted. But BT wasn't interested in the hare and was soon romping up the hill after the Floosie, his feet no longer bothering him. Now, he had to be persuaded back home at night.

Eventually, the call went out, 'Have you seen BT?' and despite searching high and low, he was never seen again. We were all very sad but knew that his time with us had been real quality for the rabbit, and for us. He had a freedom he loved, only bit those who truly annoyed him, and had BT chuckling all the way to the bank with his passion for telephone cables. He had enjoyed the company of another rabbit, as well as Felix who became very fond of him, and in the end, left a huge gap in our lives. That winter Felix succumbed to old age and left a bigger gap in our lives.

'The house isn't right,' Connie insisted as she looked around the animal-free kitchen. Indeed, it was many long years since The Sheiling ran without the joy of having a house pet, though we still had the horses and the sheep.

Maybe Benjamin BT took to the road again, feet fixed and on his way to a new life. We liked to think that, but there was always the possibility the fox got him, as Connie had so often warned. The hare was killed on the road and The Floosie lost all interest in our garden.

Long before BT, the braes at the back had one particularly big warren with several entrances right in the middle, and a few burrows round the edges of the brae where we saw foxes now and again. In *Heads on Pillows* I told the story of my inordinate embarrassment when I called a table full of excited guests from their breakfast to see the lovely fox lying in the sun on the top of the brae not far from where whins grew in profusion. They were all so excited, their rapidly cooling food of no importance. It was only when the fox moved I realised it was next door's rarely seen, very large, very fluffy, red cat, with its long extra-ordinarily bushy red tail.

I managed to shoo them back to the table before they too cottoned on to the reason for a face that was turning as red as the cat's fur!

On another occasion we had reason to watch a fox with a temperament that proved as fiery as his colouring. This excerpt taken from *Bye Bye B&B* tells the circumstances.

One afternoon, in our kitchen overlooking the braes where the big, fat, wild rabbits, spoiled by my protection from antagonists, enjoyed their main warren, we watched as a fox came down to the perimeter fence behind our house in pursuit of a juicy rabbit. Himself told me he had one day watched, mesmerised, as the very same fox crept almost up to our back green and as quick as a flash, snaffled a rabbit in the blink of an eye. The poor bunny didn't know what hit him. I remonstrated, on behalf of our latest house rabbit, Jettison. Those were her friends! I was firmly told to leave the wildlife to get on with what was natural to them and observe without interference.

Now I had the opportunity. This was as close as I ever saw Raynard on the land in daylight. The rabbit shot down a burrow. I cheered. The fox rampaged about for a bit then began, in the most aggressive manner, to dig at the burrow, hind quarters up in the air and front paws going like pistons.

It was a beautiful afternoon and the sun glinted off his russet rear, his fabulous brush bobbing up and down in his efforts to get at his prey. The grass on the braes, kept short by the nibbling of rabbits and cropping of horses and sheep, was sharp and green in contrast to his coat. The horses and sheep had moved pastures a good week before, so none disturbed the intensity of his ferocious attack on the burrow. Despite the beauty of the hunter and his determination, I was rooting for the rabbit, but I think Himself hoped the fox would be the victor.

Being married a long time now, we knew not to air our differences unless necessity demanded, so we watched, fascinated, in silence. Raynard would dig a bit, stop, listen, then run a little to where another outlet must have been, ears intently forward giving his movements a fervour suited to a fox. Then back to the digging. He was convinced Peter Rabbit would pop out the other bolt hole, keeping more of an eye on it than the area of digging. He got more and more frustrated when this did not happen.

Eventually, between bouts of digging and checking the bolt hole, he bit off chunks of turf in a towering rage, threw pieces all over the place, high into the air in his angst. Just when he moved to closely inspect the burrow's back door, Peter Rabbit shot out of the hole the fox had dug so wide. Up the hill raced Peter to the big warren, jet propelled, accompanied by my shouts of, 'Good on you, rabbit!' I had kept silent long enough. Himself gave me a dignified dirty look.

This was one of my house-rabbit's pals, after all. The fox now had no chance, so deep was the main warren, and full of very large bold rabbits. I thought it quite hilarious; it certainly was not common to see a fox in the fields so close to the house.

And so back to the fox who took over The Sheiling, dressed as she was, in a black and white coat. She was still a kitten when Neil came in one day to say he had found a feral grey-striped cat in the stable, with kittens! Were they small enough to be tamed?

'I don't think so. I've seen the cat around and she's very shy, but I'll take them some food.' It was early summer and the horses had open stabling, going in as often as not to avoid a hot day. The cat had her kittens in a hay nest tucked into a crevice in the wide stone walls easily hosting enough nooks and crannies to hide a bed of kittens.

After a few weeks the cat appeared close to the house with her brood, one red fluffy kitten we called Rob Roy, after the red haired Scottish hero, Rob Roy MacGregor; a black and white we later learned was the image of her father, and a pale grey and white kitten, not dark striped like the mother. Naturally, we called the mother Mrs MacGregor. In time we saw the father, a real beauty we called Big Tom. We began to feed the ferals regularly, never at that time hearing of Cats Protection. Smudge soon spotted them and kept a fascinated vigil. Then she saw Big Tom. If only she continued to keep her distance, a lot of trouble could have been avoided.

This was around the time Anne stopped coming to stay, her and Neil having parted, leaving Smudge with a gap to fill. She did this by falling completely in love with Big Tom. It was the first of many boyfriends, and trouble came with them all. She was completely besotted with him. If she spotted him around, she was out the door, stalking, waiting until she was sure he was on his own, then approaching. He did nothing to deter her.

Mrs MacGregor took extreme exception to such behaviour and who would blame her. Any time she saw Smudge, she went for her, and she was a big, angry cat. Smudge travelled everywhere with me now, never leaving her at home alone. She loved to walk and had been following us all over the lands for many weeks before Mrs MacGregor made her appearance. No matter what I was doing, about midmorning Smudge would sit at the back door and spring into action making for the front of the house, or the side gate to the hill, each time I appeared. I was meant to follow her, and did so when I could. The walk could be through the hills, half a mile or so to Barbara's, Himself's sister, or it could be to the riverside, but she never liked the sand that fringed the river and kept always to the tussocky grass.

We remembered how Felix had been hit on the road and left lying there for dead and though The Sheiling was set off the road, I found the soft felt harness Bendy wore when he walked out after his myxomatosis and surprise, surprise, Smudge loved to walk on the lead. At that time, emails were not the standard communication and each night I had letters to post, Himself, when at home, would set off – in the dark mind you – with his cat on a lead to post the letters. I just wish his mates on the oil rig could have seen him!

Of course, such practice had to throw up a googly with Smudge involved.

I went to the Post Office frequently very much liking Evelyn, a young German woman who ran it. The office was tiny, enough room only for a couple on the customer side of the counter, with more room for Evelyn on the official side. To the left was the area the postmen used to sort the mail, perfectly roomy and with the door always open. The building was quite old, had indeed been the cosy home of a distant relative of my own, long before I came to the village, and on one side there were outbuildings. Smudge took to visiting on her own, and being such a fine hunting feline, fond of Evelyn too, she kept the place vermin free. No problem then? As if!

'Joan, you must stop Smudge from coming here,' Evelyn demanded in the Germanic way of coming straight out with things, as I stood at the counter on my own, except of course for Smudge who trotted down the road with me, having had her Green Cross Code training, was expert at staying on pavements and not crossing the road until completely free of traffic. She had long since ditched the harness and lead.

'What's she done now?' What could she have done I wondered as I looked down on her, sitting there patiently, all innocence.

'She's scaring the customers!'

'What?'

'Oh, it's not really her fault but there's been complaints. She hunts here you know. Well, every time she gets a mouse, no matter who's in, she takes it in and you have no idea how many people scream and rush into the postmen's room. She's been known to leap on the counter to drop a bloody mouse on people's papers.'

'At least they're dead.' That paragon of virtue, Felix, used to bring in her mice, alive, especially when Barbara Jappy was in the kitchen and drop them at her feet. Barbara went absolutely mental, screaming, leaping on chairs, and refusing to move until she had a signed agreement that the mouse had been caught, and removed from the scene, far removed! Disabled with laughter, it took time to get back to normal.

Evelyn sighed. 'Ah! But sometimes they're not dead.' She didn't have to say more. I promised to try and keep Smudge away and she promised to ensure the cat no longer got a welcome. Funnily enough, this was achieved, by Mrs MacGregor and her mate keeping Smudge engrossed in her own grounds.

Some weeks before then, the weather turning cold that day, I was about to light the fire when the phone rang. Our neighbour across the road, Betty, was extremely deaf so hated using the phone, but the moment I picked up, her voice shouted down the line, 'Joan, don't light your fire.'

'What?' I mean, how did she know I was going to light the fire. She was at least 100 metres away and though we had huge windows, no way was Betty doing a bit of a spying act. She carried on, 'Your kitten. I came back from walking the dog and could see this little thing prancing about your roof. By the time I reached home, she's sitting looking down the chimney.'

I conveyed a hurried thanks and rushed outside. How could she have got up there? She was so tiny, she could fall down the chimney. Once before we had lost a gorgeous grey kitten, couldn't find it anywhere. Our fuel was predominantly peat which gives a fine red ash and I was about to light the fire when this uneasy feeling came over me. There was no reason on this earth why I should think the kitten was up the chimney, but I felt round all the ledges and could not believe it when my fingers touched a warm fluffy bundle. She was completely red with ash and very sorry for herself. The fact something had made me check up there before lighting the fire was as much a puzzle as a relief. She had been missing for some time and we could only think the vacuum had scared her, but what an escape.

'Smudge, come back down here at once!' I yelled, wondering how. Walking all round the house I saw nothing had been left, no ladder that she could have used. I needn't have worried. She literally skipped off the pot, leaped on to the ridge, raced across it, slithered down the tiles, and swung off the guttering, felt about with her back legs while my heart stood still. It was a good drop and I hovered below with my arms spread wide. Once she gripped the harling, no problem, she scrabbled down backwards. She'd done this before!

Later, when Himself was doing maintenance that required a ladder, or cleaning the chimney, Smudge was his right hand 'man', but unlike her backwards swing to get down the harling, she always rushed down the ladder head first. For a long time we checked the roof before lighting the fire. However, she seldom failed to turn up for lunch and dinner and throughout her life made sure she had three square meals a day, making sure there was a light supper to see her through the night. Leading such exciting days required high maintenance!

One evening we headed off for the night to the Portland Arms Hotel, meeting our friends John and Ishbel to attend a dinner-dance. Smudge had all her necessities in the car and would sleep quite safely, parked as we were, close to the entrance. Straight after dinner, I told Ishbel I'd go and take Smudge for a quick run out. She and John had their two dogs to attend so I was back much quicker. Immediately a member of staff grabbed me. 'Is it your cat? Oh, she's just gorgeous and you must take her in. Honestly, it will be fine.'

There was another big event in the hotel but that dining room was now cleared and people had been milling in and out for ages. Smudge, of course, played to the gallery, apparently so many people chatting to her through the car window, I said, OK, I'd take her to the room out of the way. Taking no chances, I put her on the lead, grabbed her bed and bin and started to climb the stairs when a chap who'd been to the other event, shouted up, 'I've seen it all now. I've heard of people taking their dogs on holiday, but a cat!'

'Hush!' I stage-whispered back, 'She's convinced she's a dog.'

Smudge was high on excitement, though not quite wagging her tail, all these people making a fuss of her, and now getting in among them all. What fun!

Back in the bedroom, just as I was about to go back to the function hall, Ishbel came in from walking the dogs. Smudge saw her chance and dashed out the open door. We both chased after her, along the corridor and down the staircase. She scooted into the large empty dining room, lit only from the hallway. I can't tell you how many tables I crawled under while she took the place by storm, convinced this was the best ever 'I see you' played. I was totally exasperated. Eventually I caught her, carried her back to the room and closed the door, leaning on it, saying quietly to Ishbel, 'The little bitch!'

'Cats! You should have got a dog.' She was a confirmed dog person.

It would have been the small hours of the morning before we got back to the room. Our half-grown cat looked so sweet, sound asleep with paws round Fox. I would have forgiven her anything. Her bin had not been used, but about six o'clock I heard the rustle and thought, she's bound to come into the bed, never having slept in a bedroom before. But not Smudge, no, the four-poster was tested out as a climbing apparatus. It was one with a canopy top and she pounced all over this, peeking over the edges to look at us, then racing up and down the posts, swinging on the canopy. She went ballistic. Desperately tired, I hauled on clothes and got her back to the car where she was obliged to stay until we left.

The Portland Arms is totally changed now, but in its day, with Jerry and Helen Henderson as owners, it was the place to be and Smudge ensured she made excellent use of her opportunity to sample the best. I now work with their lovely daughter-in-law, Angela, as volunteers with Cats Protection. When you live in areas like this, it can be a very small world.

Chapter 21

'Be wary of a horse with a sense of humour.'

Pam Brown

A Horse Takes Over The Reins

We set off to look for a riding horse for me and a companion for Troubie, after we sent back to Alice and John their evil little stallion, much better behaved than when he arrived. Troubie was now a loner, except when going out with the local girls, several of them now proud owners of better behaved Shetlands than Pixy. My first search for a riding horse was in Caithness. Not finding any for sale closer to home, Janet heard of a suitable animal that lived much further south, a part-Highland, part Thoroughbred, 16hh dun coloured gelding, sturdy enough to require no stabling where he lived. Perfect.

We set off to meet this horse, Himself immediately sussing out something was not quite what it should be when the owner's wife looked on very anxiously from the farmhouse window as I mounted Bronco. I was not impressed with the name. It was explained that the horse was much loved but he was escaping from his field and doing his own thing, hence the long newly healing scar on his foreleg, caught in wire, added to the fence in the hope he would not attempt another jump. For his own sake he had to go. Seemed a reasonable reason for selling a fine young horse.

There was more to the story but it was a long time before I sussed it out. Apparently his owner had his own special reason to ride the horse to the local hostelry, ran by an attractive young woman, and Bronco thoroughly enjoyed the pint of Tennant's Beer he was bribed with to await his master.

Nor was I told that his master, who was a bit of a wheeler and dealer in animals, met Bronco en route to the knacker's yard because of his dangerous behaviour. He didn't believe this three year old, soft-eyed, friendly animal should suffer such a fate and took him off his owner's hands. The horse was great, I was told, except for the escape tendencies, coupled now with a love of Tennant's. So when things changed and his trips to the pub were curtailed, Bronco did not like it and jumped fences to make his own way to get his pint. Calls came to collect the horse when he refused to budge without his chosen beverage so this embarrassing reminder of his master's peccadillo meant Bronco had to go.

The name too. It should have made me think. He gave a few bucks, but nothing I couldn't handle and, in truth, it was love at first sight. However, Bronco made his first mistake by shoving Himself out of the way, lashing out with a front hoof and ripping his jacket pocket wide open.

'Oh, he's just looking for sugar lumps, a bad habit,' the farmer immediately put in. As it happened, he never again 'looked for sugar lumps' but could lift his feet with the best of them, though I didn't know that, so purchase was agreed, transport arranged and the great day arrived, access park closed off with the two-year old Troubie looking on from the other side of the park. One never knew how animals, like people, would take to each other.

A massive horse box drew in and the driver warned that Bronco created hell when he was tied but travelled perfectly, all the way…loose! Not advisable, but there you go. He came prancing off the box, dancing and snorting. It was not the best of times to take in a new horse, early winter, but the best of times when getting rid of one! His coat was thicker and a darker dun, and he looked that bit heavier than when I had my last sight of him, racing up to the top of the only hill in his park, standing there with his main blowing in the breeze, tail flowing out behind him, watching us intently as we drove away. I was convinced he knew.

Troubie screamed out a high pitched neigh and Bronco shot off to accost him over the fence. They sniffed and snorted, hackles raised, then both went to the gate, standing quietly each side of it. It's probably our ignorance that allowed me open the gate and let them at each other. It was an immediate acceptance, racing round and round the park together, each showing their high stepping abilities, tails arched and heads held tight. In the years to come, that became their race track, showing off so often in front of The Sheiling window, to all the guests. Troubie just adored Bronco from the word go and gave in to him in everything. The first hurdle was over. Next, the stable.

There was no problem getting a head collar on the new horse, but each time Himself came near, Bronco shoved him away, so I was left to it. I led him to the stable door, low in access then, no problem for the smaller Troubie, but no way would Bronco lower his head to go in. We had made another loose box with hay rack waiting for him, but he was not going in and when he said, no, he meant, no. Himself had to come back.

'You lead Troubie in and I'll follow with Bronco,' I suggested. If Troubie was led in once he was led in a dozen times, but no way would Bronco follow. Himself, whose patience is far above mine, gave up. Troubie, bless his little white socks, started leading Bronco in by himself, and every time Bronco refused, Troubie tried again. Darkness fell, and hunger gnawed, and I wondered if we would have to give over a space in the large barn to the horse. He may have been OK out in a field further south, but not during one of our winter nights, not with his thoroughbred genes weakening the strong Highland propensity to stand the cold with only a good shelter.

At long last, Bronco made his move, eyes rolling and feet stamping, he went into a loose box, facing the one Troubie was in so they could look at each other through the bars. Troubie's was not an expressive face, but I'm sure if he could have, he'd have done a high five with Bronco, he was so pleased at achieving what instinct told him was necessary.

Next night, when I collared them for stabling Bronco went in first and made straight for Troubie's loose box. It was that bit bigger and made sense but how had they came to that conclusion as that is the way it stayed, and trespassing in another's loose box became a crime punishable by a bite. Bronco, all his life, went into the stable first, and never gave way to any other horse, except for Behan. He had a profound respect, as we all had, for Behan.

We had hoped Himself would also ride the horse, and I could use Troubie when Neil, who was by now six years old, did not ride him. Troubie was just over two years old and until then we had walked the pony on his lead all over the beaches and hills, appreciating he could not be ridden properly until much older, so he went out with us like a dog and became well acquainted with the area.

It was time for Bronco to start learning too so one lovely day my unimpressed husband and I set off with the horse to the beach. I rode Bronco while Himself walked. No problem. On the beach, my husband went to get into the saddle and all hell let loose. Bronco went mental. No way was this man getting on his back. Why, I don't know, he had been ridden by a man, so it wasn't a male phobia. I yet had to take him out on my own, but what was this all about. After several fruitless attempts while the horse bucked and reared and raced round me in circles as I held on to the leading rein, Himself called him some very fine words and left it at that. His riding days were over before they started. Bronco calmed down, I got back on his sweating back and we walked sedately home. In years to come, Smudge's first sensible action in our home was to make a fuss of Himself. See how that paid off. And we're supposed to believe horses have superior sense. No way.

And this mad horse had no aversion to walking out with a cat riding on his back. This was Samantha, another black and white cat who courted trouble. She, along with her siblings arrived one night astonishing us into the knowledge we did not have a male cat in our two year old Felix. This came as more of a shock than a surprise!

After the disappearance of Puss-do, I vowed, no more cats. But Neil kept asking for a kitten and in a moment of weakness, I said, 'OK. If you can find a jet black, male, kitten.' In no time, he and Ellis walked in with a jet black kitten we were assured was a tom, born to Ciss's queen who assiduously supplied the village with her progeny. At that time, black cats were not common and I never for a moment believed Neil could find one. As it happened, he was hiding the white hairs under the cat's chin with one hand and the tiny white patch on her tummy with the other hand. Felix was a firm favourite and when she disappeared for a couple of days, we were very afraid she was gone for good.

We were testing out the facilities in room three, as we did from time to time, prior to opening the season with Neil upstairs in his twin room. In the middle of the night I heard him racing downstairs, shouting, 'I can hear Felix.'

The meows came from the cupboard under the stairs and in its depth we saw two luminous eyes shining in the torchlight. 'What's he doing in there?' I gasped as the cat shot past me and raced for the door. I let him out into the garden and he headed for the bushes, piddle dripping from our lovely tom cat. Before he completed the job he raced past me and straight back into the cupboard. I crawled in and could not believe my eyes. There were three newly born kittens tucked up in the mound of wool and half completed garments I was assuring myself I would finish knitting…some day. This was no tom cat!

To my great relief, a home was found for all the kittens, even the black and white Samantha who had caused so much trouble being returned twice before finding the best of homes.

My life with Bronco was only just starting, a relationship that lasted for more than a quarter century and ended in a misery I was never able to speak of for years and still hurts to think about it. Bronco makes his appearances in both *Heads on Pillows* and *Bye Bye B&B* and although the lead horse in my adventure novel, *The Land Beyond The Green Fields*, was not based on Bronco, his character certainly had a walk-on part in the steed belonging to the master of the hunt.

Today our stable is empty of horses, even though Neil heightened and renovated the building in the hope that the early interest in ponies shown by Shane and later by Fallon would see horses back on the land, but that did not happen. Instead, there is firewood stored in the stable and cattle roaming the fields, a cockerel and his little entourage of hens scrabbling about the braes. I am frequently seen walking a large chocolate Labrador, and of late, enticing a tiny black Labrador puppy to do its duty in the garden across the road, or our garden during Misty's frequent sojourns up here, much to the chagrin of Poodie, who carries her aversion to our family right through to include their animals.

How do these adverse plans come about, I often wonder, because I have no recollection of being in on the decisions, I sympathise with the cat as I did not expect to have dogs, hens, or cows, in these, my so-called retirement years. I suppose they think retirement is a joke as I rush about, working with the Federation of Small Businesses, the Highlands & Islands Tourism Awards Board, and of course, my writing, all of which require a fair bit of travel, living as we do, on the edge of the land, and so much happening way down that road making sure I spend as much time in the car as I do at any meeting or talk. And, like most jobs taken on by me anyway, I always believe there will be little work involved, like Cats

Protection. It's like Topsy, continuous growth and no antidote I can bring into effect, to date.

I never seem to be out of the car, heading here, there and everywhere, so I wonder too, how people did so much when they had only the horse to aid their mobility.

Chapter 22

'A cat is more intelligent than people think, and can be taught any crime.'

Mark Twain

The Cat Who Cared

'What are you going to do then?' Connie asked, looking out the window at Mrs MacGregor and her growing brood. 'We can't keep Smudgie under our eye all the time and what happened to her yesterday was terrible.'

Yesterday! Connie had gone home and I was busy in the kitchen when a guest rushed in with a battered looking Smudge in her arms. 'We looked out the window and that dreadful cat had Smudge by the throat,' she gasped out. 'She would have killed her, you know, if I hadn't banged on the window and rushed out.'

Yes, I did know, and it was becoming a big problem. Smudge was hell bent on getting Big Tom for herself, stalking him while trying to keep out of Mrs MacGregor's way, not in the least interested in the trio of kittens. Then, at her last check at the vet's another decision had to be made. 'I've heard it's good for cats like Smudge to have kittens. Settles them down,' I tentatively suggested.

'A myth,' the vet answered. 'I'd have her spayed as soon as possible.' Was he seeing the glint in her eye when she thought of Big Tom? I took her home, warning her to stay away from trouble.

I did not follow the vet's sensible advice and quickly ascertained, while Smudge was exuding charm in equal measure to naughtiness, that I could find homes for this prospective litter. It would be two years down the line before that litter appeared. The mayhem she created over their birth saw me sallying forth to that self-same vet, a wiser and more humbled owner, Smudge and her growing offspring, all still under her rule and all booked to ensure that neither she nor they would be replicating their maternal genes – my reputation would not stand another Smudge in the community.

But for now, Smudge was the new innocent kitten, delighting all our guests.

'Isn't she sweet,' Joyce Savage smiled when we arrived back at the house. Bill and Joyce had been with us for their usual few days and loved nothing better than taking Smudge for a walk, delighted that Felix had a lively and interesting successor. They were leaving in the morning. As I unloaded the groceries, the Savages went off up the hill with Smudge prancing ahead of them. She was going to miss them every bit as much as I would.

Just before dinner a very upset couple found Connie and I in the kitchen. They had lost Smudge. Mrs MacGregor had flown out of the whins at the top of the brae, Smudge took off and no amount of searching could find her.

'Don't worry, she'll come home herself,' I assured them. Though far from fully grown, she was much bigger now and roamed at will. She'd be fine, I told myself. 'But are you going to have her spayed, and what are you going to do about Mrs MacGregor?' Connie persisted as she got out of the car at her house with no Smudge to tempt the barking dogs.

'I'm not sure about spaying, Connie, but you said there's this Cats Protection I can get a trap from. I think we'll have to get all those ferals neutered. In fact, the kittens are coming closer and closer to us. We may yet be able to home them.'

Next morning there was no sign of Smudge and the Savages delayed their departure, determined to find her, but failing miserably, they set off south. Every few hours a phone call came, not from a mobile, having no such facility then, but from wherever they stopped for a break. 'Is she back yet?' their anxious voices came down the line.

I felt so bad, saying no, and please don't worry, she'll be fine while at the same time sick with worry, convinced Mrs MacGregor had got her this time. Despite Smudge's behaviour, we all loved her to bits, but we knew keeping her indoors in a busy household was not an option, especially a cat who loved being outdoors. She would have to learn the dangers, and we would have to help by doing something about Mrs MacGregor, if only Smudge would come home.

And she did. She came skipping across the green next morning, happy as a sand boy with Big Tom in tow. The Savages were mightily relieved to hear the outcome, promising to come back next year. We loved them dearly and hated to give them so much concern. Bill has a marvellous sense of humour, and Joyce is one of the nicest people you could meet. Having them as residents always ensured a wonderful atmosphere of conviviality during their many stays at The Sheiling prompting plenty of laughs round the dining table.

Next day, with Smudge prancing about the back seat, we picked up a cat trap from a CP lady called Sandra who had loads of cats, but she'd have taken Smudge too judging by her interest. If Connie hadn't been with me, I might have said, 'Yes please, take her! She's nothing but a bundle of trouble.'

But she was far more than that, Himself so deeply fond of her he took full charge of setting the trap that night for whatever cat we could get, after making sure Smudge was tucked up in her igloo with Fox. We were like two excited kids when we heard the bang of the trap door closing about three in the morning.

It was Big Tom himself, and in to the vet he went. He was far from being amused but we were delighted. A couple of nights later we caught Mrs MacGregor. Brilliant! Cats Protection made the appointment to have all three kittens done at once since we proved so adept at trapping. I knew Connie would help as Himself had gone back to the rig.

The trap was set the night before, and in the morning, there was Rob Roy. I always felt sorry for this red kitten. His mother favoured what turned out to be the two females, one grey striped with white, the other black and white, the spitting image of Big Tom. When Rob Roy tried to eat, his mother hissed at him, yet let the girls eat their fill. We decanted him into the wicker basket and set the trap again. In no time we had the grey kitten. Very encouraging, we agreed. Connie had the rooms almost ready and I had most of the prep for dinner near completion so all we had to do was catch the last kitten, get them all back into the trap, and off to the vet. Simples! Or so we thought.

At that time there was no problem with appointments. CP gave you a trap and authorised the operation with the vet and you caught the cats when you could, taking them in for neutering after a quick phone call to say you'd be in that day. An appointment was made for the kittens because three were a lot to take in at the same time. It's a different story today and much more difficult to synchronise as you must have a definite appointment for a feral and have the cat at the vet's at 9am, no argument! There's never a guarantee of a catch but the appointment is essential as phoning unexpectedly with a feral means being turned away, so no point. So, when you have – as I have at this moment – four traps in various villages trying to catch four particularly difficult roving toms, it can be soul destroying to make these appointments, guessing at a possible two cats being caught, but then what if you get three, though more than often it is none, which means cancelling the appointment and trying again. The vets' patience is admirable, mine is debatable, as for the cats, they have no patience whatsoever for any of this. Yet, after the deed is done, it is surprising the glossy creatures who turn up expecting their dinner to be laid on, their well-being so improved, they allow a certain amount of interaction with the people who feed them and will even condescend to coming into to the house, two now locally taking over the homesteads as 'their' cats!

Thankfully, we had no such problem with appointments at that time, and reset the trap by the peat shed for the last feral kitten, ears attuned for the clang of the door snapping shut. It was some time before the black and white kitten arrived, attracted by the smell of cat meat. All was quiet and another look proved Big Tom was now with his daughter. Each time she approached the trap, he hissed at her.

We watched in disbelief, yet fascinated.

It became very clear Big Tom had no intention of allowing this kitten into that trap, no matter she was desperate to get at the food. He circled round and round the trap, keeping her well away from it, nor did he attempt to go in there himself. He'd done that and known the consequences!

Connie got her tuppence-worth in, 'No problem, until this one. Typical. A black and white kitten and a black and white father. We may as well give up.' She was not the giving-up type, so I ignored her.

We put cream and a little roast chicken, a firm favourite, in the trap. No use. Big Tom kept on circling each time the kitten showed an interest. I opened a tin of sardines. Mrs MacGregor was nowhere to be seen but the two kittens locked up in the garage were protesting their incarceration with howls that grew louder by the minute. Sardines did not do the trick.

As usual, my patience gave way first. 'I can't wait any longer. We're going to have to take those two in Connie.'

A steely determination came over her face. 'You leave it to me. I'm going to get that kitten once and for all! I've been having a think about this, and there's no way I'm letting a black and white cat get the better of me, so there!'

How? I wondered as she headed for the garage.

Back Connie came, smiling, and was barely in the door when bang! I raced out and there was the kitten in the trap and Big Tom nowhere to be seen.

'On earth, what did you do?' I gasped out.

'I took a kipper from the freezer. I put half in the trap and the other half over the fence. The minute Big Tom took off after the kipper, the kitten went into the trap.' We laughed, delighted to have outwitted him.

The deed was done, the kittens now much quieter as we drove them home. We managed to do as the vet advised, let the male kitten out, keeping the girls in for a longer recovery. The young tom streaked off in a flurry of red fur. The females then began the most mournful caterwauling you ever heard. I have a photograph of the young Smudge, curiously staring at the kittens in the trap. She was intrigued but took off when Rob Roy made his sprint for freedom. We moved the trap into the patio in the hope that seeing their natural surroundings would quieten them or at least get their mother to come and comfort them.

I've since learned of the amazing solace feral cats bring to an incarcerated member of their tribe, mothers especially, sometimes siblings lying close to the covered cage to comfort the incumbent while waiting for the pick-up to go to the vet. They are often there, waiting for the return and only run off when the spayed cat runs with them. These stories come from many of the people who feed ferals and help to get them neutered, help that makes the job so much easier.

But this time it was our kittens' father who showed up, very annoyed at what was going on. He set about pawing the wires of the trap, in a desperate bid to get his daughters out.

Mrs MacGregor took no heed whatsoever of the cries for help yet Big Tom began to howl too, both he and the kittens making such a scene we had to let them out, and away they sped with their diligent father, seemingly none the worse for their ordeal. Connie and I were absolutely shattered!

We continued to befriend the kittens and got homes for the two females on a farm at Dounreay. Mrs MacGregor got even meaner to Rob Roy until one day we saw her walking up the hill with him. They were gone for about four days, days of great joy for Smudge as she solidified her relationship with Big Tom. Like many a male before him, he seemed to think he could have both Mrs MacGregor and his bit on the side! Mrs MacGregor had other ideas, newly returned and ready for war, but we never saw Rob Roy again.

Mmm…I thought. Mrs MacGregor's doing a bit of forward planning, having taken her son into other territory! Looked like I too would have to initiate some forward thinking if Smudge were ever to grow up in peace.

I went back to Sandra for a loan of the trap and did what I now know from my work with Cats Protection, no lover of animals should do, and CP most decidedly does not approve. I trapped Mrs MacGregor and took her far away from our Smudge, ensuring I put her in a place with trees, rabbits, water, where rough vegetation grew not too far from habitation and with plenty of good hunting. I was told it was a place where there were no feral cats in the vicinity.

I wished her well, for I truly did not know what else to do for the safety of my mad kitten. I appreciated that Mrs MacGregor deserved a good hunting area, but it was not of her own choosing. For a long time I wondered if she would do what many cats did, and find her way back.

In truth, I was mightily relieved to be free of such a ferocious creature. I salved my conscience believing she was bad to her son, and didn't care about her daughters crying for help. It was their father who showed his paternal care. We continued to feed and care for this beautiful tom cat, but we never ever got near him. Not like Smudge.

She was now free to pursue her romance with the love of her young life. She was totally besotted with him, and when Connie arrived with the unexpected gift of Jettison, Smudge

209

had little interest in the rabbit which was really surprising as she was turning into a formidable little hunter.

Big Tom was seen around with Smudge so great care was taken in keeping an eye on Jettison. She grew into a beautiful, fine looking rabbit and when the weather suddenly turned hot, Neil and Ellis put up an enclosure round a tree in the back garden for her to play in comparative safety. We have a series of pictures of Smudge sitting on the fencing watching Jettison, then jumping in beside her. You see clearly from those pictures that in short order, Jettison sent Smudge packing from her playground. She was indeed a feisty rabbit, not quite as dominant as Bendy and nowhere near as naughty as Rex. But she was going to look after her own affairs, she made clear to the indignant young cat who pretended it was all part of a big game.

Then one quiet spring day when Smudge was only a few months old, I said to Connie, 'Do you think there's something wrong with Smudge? She's so quiet. Hasn't done anything rotten to anyone for days and she's not asking to play hide and seek. Nor is she plaguing me to take her walks. I wonder what's bothering her?'

'She's not eating properly either,' Connie observed. Smudge took her milk and porridge in the mornings, but no more soups for lunch, or meat and two veg for dinner. She got quieter and quieter, then one day Usdean next door mentioned he had found a beautiful big black and white cat dead in one of the old outhouses. It must have been Big Tom as we never saw him again. Smudge was bereft and now we guessed why.

Yet, after a couple of weeks of being miserable, she was back to her usual tricks and we wondered was it coincidence or did she really mourn the death of her suitor. Today we have irrefutable evidence of how the death of a lifelong companion can affect an animal. Thankfully, Smudge began to eat cat food, except for breakfast, and insisted she be fed at lunch, dinner and supper time, her pleas to eat when we did coming without a single meow passing her lips. And no matter how we tried, we could never persuade her to sit on a lap.

Then she disappeared, off the face of the earth, and no amount of searching or calling could find her.

Chapter 23

*'Dogs come when they're called; cats take a message
and get back to you later.'*

Mary Bly

The Cat Came Back

'Is she back yet?' It was the first thing Connie asked every morning as she came on duty, and every morning I shook my head.

'I've searched day and night. We've all searched. Mind you, getting a hold of Neil is like trying to catch the wind. He's hardly here, is he? He's up to something, Connie, isn't he?'

'You're fishing, what you are. Well, I'm not telling, what I'm not!' She had a smug look on her face.

'There's a girl in this, somewhere, isn't there. I'm told nothing. And this time he needn't smart-ass me with, 'You never asked.' I ask plenty, but no way is he saying.'

'Well then, I'm not saying either, and I have work to do!' She was off, no point pursuing it. I would find out in good time.

And I did. Early one morning I spotted the top of a female head bobbing past the kitchen window and I was just too slow to see the rest of its owner before I heard a car start up. Neil had yet to appear in the kitchen and I had a busy household to see to. Still idly puzzling over the owner of the dark-haired head, right in the middle of preparing breakfast, the phone rang. Absolutely nothing unusual in that; soon it would be the doorbell, everything happening at once and as usual, before Connie arrived. I managed to answer, and heard a sob on the other end of the line. 'I need to speak to Neil.'

212

'What's wrong?' It seemed natural to ask.

'I crashed my car and I want to speak to Neil…now!'

I didn't know who she was, but my first concern was, 'Are you all right? I'm on my way to get him.' She wasn't hurt and who she was, I didn't have a clue, but she was obviously very shaken, and so was I now, full of questions that would have to wait.

Those of us who are used to driving in our area know black ice can be an early morning hazard and this young lady had demolished a stone bridge en route to her work in Thurso.

Was she driving a tank!

Recovering from his shock, Neil rushed off and brought back to our home the first official visit of his new girlfriend, the previous night being unexpected after a late night party out west. This was Katrina Geddes, and we decided we would just keep her, forever, despite the nerve-wracking introduction. I took to her immediately, but Smudge did not. Not that Smudge was back home, and that may have been part of her angst: this new female getting her feet under the table and attracting all the attention while she was off on her first venture into the unknown! How dare this happen in her absence!

My mind was filled with the disappearance of Smudge and the natural inquisitiveness of a mother who knows her son is taking a serious interest in a girl, especially when that mother would have liked nothing better than a girl of her own. Would this Katrina become that person? I had kept in touch with Anne although the romance was well and truly over, and Katrina seemed to fit well into our family ways. I was happy with that instinctive knowledge, we would see a lot of Katrina. Even though life was filled with hustle and bustle, things, apart from Smudge's disappearance, were going so well. That is usually the trigger for something to go wrong!

Almost two years before that cheeky little cat entered into our lives, I had been feeling tired and unwell and had this vague feeling, for no given reason, that I had contracted breast cancer. There was no indication of such, just an instinct. Not one to go running to my doctor, except for the excruciating migraines I had suffered since 11 years old, my fears were heeded and an appointment made at the breast unit in Inverness. Examination showed no lumps or bumps, but calcification showed up on a mammogram that required 'watching.' I diligently went every now and again when called for a check-up. Then, after being persuaded by new guests I got to know, to try a long course of liquid Aloe Vera, my health began to pick up considerably and as the months rolled on, I started to put appointments off until I found time to pick them up. I was convinced I was fine.

Delighted though I was to welcome Katrina and all else going extremely well in both work and play, at the back of my mind was the guilt that I'd put off what I was assured would be my final check-up because nothing had changed, and now, turning 50, I could go on to the usual routine for my age and attend the mobile unit that came into our area. So with little thought, I put off an appointment for the second time. However, a call from the clinic nurse persuading me I really ought to take this opportunity, just so they could say goodbye to me. I'd been seeing them for about two years by now and after this scan they'd be happy to hand me over to the normal mammogram programme for women of my age.

Agreeing to an appointment the following week suited my schedule. I had at last organised a holiday, another safari in East Africa, and attached to this was a week in Madagascar to see the lemurs. I was so excited about going to see these fascinating animals, I thought of little else as I drove through Strath Halladale that morning. In my bag was the money for the holiday to pay the travel agent in Inverness as we would be leaving in a couple of weeks, and I planned to buy something comfortable for travel, a suit I could make good use of again.

My mind wandered back to Smudge and what she got up to. Two long weeks after she went missing, she was still nowhere to be seen. Picking up the papers at the local shop, Barbara, the mainstay of our village grocery store, said, 'You know the man who stays in Claire's old house?'

'No,' I cut in, 'I don't know him.'

'Well, he said he had this lovely black and white cat staying with him. Came in his bedroom window one night. He said it was a lovely friendly cat and how it got up on his roof, he did not know.'

My heart leapt. It could be Smudge. Friendly? Maybe, but roof climber? Definitely! 'I'll have to go and see if it's Smudge.' Before I could get too excited, Barbara warned, 'The cat's gone now. When his son came home unexpectedly, the cat did not get on with them, and upped and off in the middle of the night, out the window she had come in, and has not been seen since. He'd really taken to her and is missing her terribly.' Apparently, the cat had been the cause of some sharp words exchanged as she let it be known she was not enamoured of this extra people in the house. That sounded just like my cat.

The upstairs bedroom wouldn't have stopped Smudge. But that house was a mile from us, in Portskerra. What on earth would have put her there? And now this cat was gone again. More searching was just as futile as before. Then one day I was setting the dining-room table for dinner for a houseful of guests, my mind full of the forth-coming holiday, when I looked out the window and saw young Carl racing through the park that separated our houses. Carl was the grandson of Barbara who had worked with me for years, living now in the home Usdean built on the next door croft to ours, with Samantha, Felix's horse-riding kitten.

I don't know why, but the delight on Carl's face as he ran towards the house had me throwing open the window, calling, 'Have you found Smudge?'

'Yes. We were going down the land to fish. Smudge was coming up through the tattie shaws, just up from the river. Grandad tried to catch her, but she ran away. He said to tell you.' It was great news, but as I was on duty with a dinner to do, no way could I leave and try to find her.

So the cat came back, waltzing in the door as if she had never been away, back in the fold, lording it over us all, taking exception to elderly ladies and making herself indispensable to all men, regardless of age.

Katrina's visits slowly increased and was viewed by Smudge with more tolerance, and the cat's propensity to pee in Neil's bags stopped. It would be good to say life went on as usual.

But it did not, not by a long chalk.

Chapter 24

'I have studied many philosophers and many cats.
The wisdom of cats is infinitely superior.'

Hippolyte Taine

Kat versus Cat!

With a frisson of excitement as I headed for Inverness, I thought over what had been an exceptionally busy year. Business was good. And it was such a beautiful morning with the sun glinting on the lochs. Both rivers flowed gently, the Halladale and the Helmsdale accompanying my journey on the single track road for 40 miles going south to meet the A9, an occasional ring of rippling water spreading outwards on the river pools, evidence of a salmon touching the surface to snatch at a hovering fly. The hills were now taking on their new mantle of purple as the mauve heather bells faded and the flowers blossomed to give this richer hue contrasting with the ferns, yet to change from their forest green to the golden bronze of early winter. It was August. I loved Sutherland in all its autumn glory every bit as much as I loved it in its raw winter wildness. I was so privileged to live where others dreamed of visiting, envying my casual familiarity with their longed for retreats. It all felt so good.

I parked and went first to choose clothes, finding a trouser suit, expensive in its natural soft fibres with enough man-made elastin to prevent crushing; to aid stretch; perfect for travel. It was an unusual shade of sea-green, almost the colour our sea takes on when the sun shines on the sandy Kyle of Tongue, the waters then darkening as clouds change the Kyle to dark turquoise before turning to grey. I was well pleased with my find. Little did I know I'd never want to wear it, and every time I saw it hanging in the wardrobe, a vague feeling of sickness would engulf me.

I happily set off to pay for our long-awaited holiday, then drove to the hospital with no thought in my head that life would never be the same again as I easily found a parking place. It wouldn't always be that easy to find parking in this increasingly busy hospital complex I would become so familiar with.

Before I knew it I had two doctors talking to me. A tiny growth had formed, not one you could easily feel, almost under my right arm. There was something about it that required urgency.

'Is there somewhere you can go until we look at this properly? If it's what we think it is, we want to do an immediate investigation. Come back in a couple of hours.'

It threw me, but what was the point in rushing off to Muriel and making a fuss. I had a huge amount of shopping for the Guest House. We were now doing dinner, bed and breakfast with several ensuite shower rooms, a large extra bathroom to suit those who liked to bath, and some time back had given over our sitting room to guests so they had two public lounges, one with TV, the other with peace to enjoy the stunning views, and to chat. After our last massive renovation I had a large kitchen with comfortable chairs, an office close by and a shower room with toilet off the back lobby, so we never had time to use the sitting room, and the guests were delighted to have a choice. This was now a much larger outfit to service. So lots of cleaning material for upkeep and lots of things to facilitate the rooms I could buy in Inverness that I could not get locally along with the usual fresh produce bought every couple of days or so.

So I shopped!

I don't know what others do in the hours waiting for possible confirmation of a life-threatening diagnosis, after getting the first indication that this is the likely outcome, but I shopped. While part of me prayed for a false alarm, the rest of me concentrated on the needs of my trade.

It was no false alarm and I returned to a meeting with three rather concerned doctors, among them a woman who did the invasive and very painful biopsy which quickly confirmed it was cancer. I was told to go home and prepare to come back into hospital in about two weeks to have the lumpectomy I agreed to after discussion. Mine was a youngish surgeon with, what I was soon to learn, a solid reputation in operating on cancer patients and it was his belief a mastectomy would not be necessary. But I could have one if that is what I wanted. Twenty years ago, things seemed to happen much quicker in the National Health.

Dr Rosemary Lee, part friend, part my GP, and a very good one at that, thought I was dicing with death. She advocated the mastectomy, and also advised me to close down my business. She knew how hard I worked. 'Give yourself a chance,' she implored.

I said no to both options. There did not seem, then, to be near so many women contracting this cancer as there are today and it shocked that I, who came across as being so fit, should be struck down with it. It was a puzzled kindness I met when word got out, but not as much encouragement as I would have liked. I could see it in people's eyes, a sympathy tinged with fear. What I really needed was a much stronger attitude as in, you have to fight this and you're the very person to do it! I have a very close friend who took exactly that line with me and it was brilliant. I hope I was as supportive with her in the months to come when she too was diagnosed with a much more advanced cancer. Proof of her fighting spirit is that today, she's still there for us to debate a tourism issue or anything else, now we are both well retired from the coal-face but still harbouring opinions of what should be and what should not be!

Himself was completely stunned, totally supportive and tried to be as positive as I felt. But Connie took it hard. I feel she never quite got over it. She was a complete treasure as we sat and discussed the future of the business in her soft, humorous way of de-stressing anxious situations. She had a way with her, appreciated so much by the people she worked along with in a career that helped many to achieve the highest of standards in servicing rooms, providing delicious food and above all, caring for customers.

For the previous couple of years Connie knew I was keen to ditch doing dinners, but my reputation was partly built on this provision. When I dared to suggest the disappearance of this service, my guests threw up their hands in horror. So I kept it going.

Now I had the best excuse in the world to drop dinners. 'There's always a silver lining', I grinned to friends who did not understand the weight of work that would be lifted from my shoulders by stopping providing those dinners. I did wonder, though, just how badly that would affect the business in an area with few eating out options unless you were prepared to get behind the wheel and drive to find a place to suit. A really good meal on the premises was most people's first choice.

Connie agreed it was best to take no more guests but honour the bookings we had, and there were many, all with dinners. But she made light of it. 'Not a problem. I'll stay here and see to the animals and the people when you're in hospital. A change is as good as a rest.' Then she added with a firm nod of the head, 'What it is!' When Connie used her favourite phrase to end a conversation, you knew all would be well.

'You can sleep in my room. It's a super-comfy bed. Mind you, you can't have it when Himself's in it.'

'You're just a meanie and a spoil-sport to boot!'

'I don't mind. Sharing is good. But people will talk.'

The arrangements slotted into place with little problem, though Jettison missed me and for the first time, started to chew electrical cables. Connie spent time searching out the misdemeanours to make furtive repairs! For Katrina, not that long arrived into our family, this was shocking news, and it is only afterwards she was able to tell me how it hit her and Neil. But they never showed it, totally positive. In an emergency, Neil's nature and training with the Marines made him the best person out to have around. Calm, cool and very collected. Wish I could say the same when he hits his thumb with a hammer, so to speak! Katrina too, coming from a military background, knew that when problems arise you deal with them. When home from the rigs, Neil spent a lot of time with Katrina who then had a flat in Scrabster and her music business in Thurso, where her parents and grandparents live. She is very much a family girl, with a sparkling personality and a great sense of humour.

My surgeon was well pleased with the fine job he made of the operation, and my hospital stay was like any other I ever had, made bearable by the rapport with patients in the same situation. At least two others shared with me a strong sense of humour as we tackled our time together, laughing until we were weak, commiserating when necessary, but agreeing, we would not keep in touch. It would be too painful to know if one or the other slipped out of the picture, a possibility hanging over all our heads.

We made the best of the craic with plenty of laughter to go along with the shared tears when we each faced different setbacks. Mine was to be told the cancer had invaded lymph nodes, many of which had been removed. It was a matter of hope that all infected nodes were gone, not a matter of certainty. There was absolutely no guarantee, so there would be no cure to boast of, merely a remission. Believe me, under these circumstances, remission is very acceptable!

However, such news is hard to take but less than five minutes after sharing the prognosis with my companions, who had their own prognosis to digest, screens drawn round each bed as different stories were sensitively divulged to each of us, Christine, one of my triplet nieces stuck her lovely head round my screen with her usual cheerful 'Hello!' then perched upon my bed and chattered nonstop until my mind digested the situation and I could still my thoughts without passing this worry on to this young woman, brimming with health and goodwill. Her exuberance for life left little time to think the worst. By the time she left, I'd got back my mojo, except I didn't know that's what it was. I just thought I was being extraordinarily positive in face of bad news! Defiantly so probably, which was part of my nature anyway.

When a child, climbing was very attractive to me. The shed roof was too tempting to resist and setting off at speed along its narrow ridge, arms outstretched to balance, eye on the barn at the end of the row of outhouses, the drop graduating higher with each step, I was so focused I almost reached my objective before I heard my mother, panting down the road from Betty's shouting, 'Get off that roof or you'll fall and be killed.' I headed back along the ridge but refused to come down from the roof where I sat for the next hour, terrified in case she carried out her threat of killing me when she got her hands on me. Hunger drove me home to a severe warning as she shook some sense into me.

'I'll kill you...' shake, shake,' 'if you ever...' shake, shake, 'if you ever put yourself in such danger again!'

I said nothing, thinking, 'I will! I will!' So now I let that mantra seep deep into my sub-conscience: 'I *will* live! I *will* live!'

I was sent home with a monumental decision to make. Would I have chemotherapy or radiotherapy? It was a big question and I did lots of research. I was strongly drawn towards radiotherapy, but a distant cousin who had a mastectomy many years before came to see me and put the fear of God into me insisting I take chemotherapy and have a full mastectomy while I had a chance, citing so many examples – she was a nurse – of why I should. I felt quite deflated, so back I went to the drawing board. I still came up with the same answers. Then my surgeon told me of a clinical trial in which I could participate. If I rang him and said I wanted to be part of this trial, it would then be a matter of phoning again and I would get the answer which came up alternatively on each call: one caller would get the chemo, the next caller, radiotherapy. A lottery! But also a trial and I was all in favour of that. Or was I just a coward, leaving such a huge decision to chance!

So I slept on it, then went for it, and next day took a big gulp, picked up the phone and was mightily relieved to hear radiotherapy come up. I felt it was right for me. The strength of that feeling was very important, and it was good to feel that in some small way I was participating in a trial that would eventually help others.

Again Dr Rosemary was mystified. She pled to have a rethink, then demand chemotherapy. I shook my head. While she admired the surgeon's work, she accepted the dye was cast as far as my surgery was concerned. In time there would be no evidence of the operation, except when décolleté was called for I'd look down, and exclaim, 'One is bigger than the other?'

Himself would do and in-depth study and respond, 'No. Doesn't look that way to me. Do I need to get my glasses on to make sure?' That was answer enough for anyone doubting their appearance!

I was convinced if I had chemotherapy, I would not survive it. Why, I don't know but every instinct told me to follow what I was doing and all would be well. Along with the radiotherapy went the oral chemical treatment. This, I found quite difficult to stand, its side effects not good, until Rosemary found me an excellent alternative but that took time. I was well settled into it when the European Union banned it. Why?

I don't know. I struggled on with the best I could tolerate, desperate for the five years to be up so I could stop it. Despite Rosemary doubting my choices, she was there to help and help she did! The first days out of hospital were a nightmare of discomfort when fluid built up under the arm, graduating to excruciating pain, the touch of even a silk nightdress unbearable, and showering became intolerable. But Rosemary was there, day or night, to drain off the fluid provided I could drive to the surgery, which I did by resting my elbow on the open car window so my upper arm did not touch my rib cage, progressing with extreme caution! Smudge was in her co-pilot position in the car before I closed the door. I was terrified she would jump out the window but she didn't like the rush of air so stayed away from the blast. I was extremely fortunate to have Dr Rosemary's understanding and diligence throughout my recovery.

Did I have Smudge's understanding during my recovery? Not her, sneaking a ride to the surgery, complaining she was hardly ever out in the car nowadays and what is wrong with you, going out in your nightdress and driving like an old lady! Her attitude was easy to read.

Her weight would thump on to the bed and a cheeky face peer at me to check if I was getting out of that bed today or tomorrow, a tentative paw poking at my eyes if I kept them closed, opening them to see a face staring at me, eyes squinting into mine, puzzled as to why I was lying there and not out going exciting walks. She was over a year old and full of herself. She'd found a new boyfriend just before I went in to hospital. A beautiful, big, healthy tomcat, dark brown and buff striped back and mask, long white legs, a white chest with white mouth and cheeks, dark brown tip to his nose. His big eyes shone clear green with a confidence unusual in a feral cat, but he was definitely not a house cat and I doubted a stray as he would not allow any approach. He came close to the house, looking very well fed and not interested in anything but

Smudge, eventually sitting on the kitchen window sill to see if she was in the kitchen. The moment you opened the door, he was gone.

But to make up for Smudge's indifference to my predicament, I had Jettison. Every day she hopped on to my bed, long black ears pinned over her back, a look of peace on her face as she snuggled up beside me. I became very attached to her and Himself gave the rabbit credit for her loyalty, pretending he didn't notice Connie's desperate bids to hide our pet's frustrated attacks on plastic wiring when I disappeared every Monday morning to get back to Inverness in time for my radiotherapy, not home again until Friday evening.

Connie coped with the depleted guest list, while I did what I could when at home and Himself did likewise, finding in Connie a great working companion. I decided to treat my hospital trips as 'my' time, do what I wanted to do, my room in the hospital annex perfectly comfortable with only a couple of other radiotherapy patients staying. We had a kitchen so I bought myself a juicer and mountains of fruit and vegetables, determined this action would help my recovery despite having a very healthy eating style anyway, apart from an inordinate love of puddings! I was lucky that my metabolism ensured no extra weight sat on my form as the years rolled by.

I had every intention of recovering and felt little need for the attentions of the MacMillan Nurse, lovely though she was and I could see each day in therapy the amount of people who relied upon her obvious skills. I was so sure all would be OK if I kept positive, filled my days with interest and let everyone else do their own thing as they saw fit.

Being completely honest I can recall some rather confusing happenings directed by people who didn't understand. Such as the nurse who arrived one afternoon on 23rd December, when I was full of the joys of the festive season, delighted I was able to do as I always did: prepare a full Christmas Dinner for Christmas Eve, entertaining at least

16 people including Connie with her favourite neice, her mother, Ciss, and Ellis, joining our extended family. One of many nurses who served the communities along the Sutherland coastline arrived unannounced, staying for absolute ages, talking more like a harbinger of doom than what I'm sure she must have intended. By the time she left, every ounce of joy was gone. What shocked was how long it took to build that feeling up again. She didn't mean it, but her determination to discuss places I'd already been, digested, made decisions and moved on. Had the offer of support and information from this source come earlier, I may have welcomed it, but at that stage, I sure as hell didn't need it. Assuming also I should have nothing better to do rather rankled, but hospitality was my game and I hadn't the heart to say, 'Will you please go and let me get on with living!' Smudge would have. Where was she when I needed her?

Eventually I managed to convey, there would be no need for such calls in the future, not unless things got as bad as she feared, and with the assurance I would ask for help when needed, I leaned on the closed door and sighed. But a shadow fell on the light that had burned so brightly.

Then there was the letter I received, with the Christmas post, telling me of many people who died of cancer, including members of their own family. Nevertheless they wished me well! That was something they never wished me before, reporting me at times when I ran seminars, and set up meetings and learning sessions for the B&B industry, but they were well known for this aggressive stance against all 'competition' regardless of coming reasonably new into both the area and the trade.

Decisions! Decisions! Would I put the letter in a frame over the fireplace, or stick it in the fire?

And getting to know Katrina was an exciting new venture too, realising how much we enjoyed each other's company, then in late summer, she brought great joy with the announcement she and Neil would be moving to Melvich and come April, we could all look forward to the patter of two tiny feet.

Once again Katrina upstaged Smudge who was trying to tell us to prepare for the patter of 16 tiny feet. We were over the moon with the prospect of a grandchild on the horizon, and happy that at last, Smudge's pregnancy slowed down her bursts of energy and she seemed to be behaving herself. Her choice of father was bound to be that fantastic feral who visited so often, and in time would prove himself to be such a gentleman.

As Katrina's bump grew, so did Smudge's and this time Smudge was determined to get in there first. Himself had by now retired from the rigs due to his growing deafness and worked with a local contractor. Then suddenly he was struck with the first real illness of his life, struggling to keep going. I was reasonably fit, but struggled with the medication and worried over our workload with sheep ready to lamb just before the season would open. We would be fine, I convinced myself, wondering would it be a boy or a girl making an appearance just before the lambs. Smudge said with a smirk, I'm bound to have both! Beat that!

The horses were seldom ridden now, Troubie's genetic fault that left him with a cannon bone perilously close to the sole of his foot was nurtured by our highly skilled blacksmith, Sandy, and meant he should only be ridden on grass, and by a light child. As for me, I never seemed to find the energy or time to take out Bronco. They were like two large pets that hankered after days gone by when their lives were much more interesting. Alice advised me that I should find an owner for Troubie, him being younger than Bronco, and with that in mind, she sent what she saw as the ideal family to come and see him.

It is well to note that two days before that Sunday visit, Smudge refused to go into her igloo, which could happen when she decided it was *unclean*!. Most cats resented their smell being replaced by fresh linen smells, our madam would never sleep in a bed used for more than a couple of weeks. But her bed was clean, to my standards, but maybe not to hers so I tried laundering it. No good.

'No? Please Smudge! Go to your bed and stop that pussy-footing about.' I got her Roxy's old basket and put it in a corner. In those days we had only the one cat bed, believing that's all a cat needed. I could not visualize the day we would need five beds to satisfy the needs of three cats, and if I'd prophesied that to Himself, he'd have had kittens…maybe not kittens but you get my drift. Anyway, Smudge accepted the basket, but she did not look comfortable. I wondered if she was planning to sneak off somewhere to have her kittens, that being the way of cats.

When the family arrived on Sunday to see Troubie, as we trooped through the kitchen to go to the stable, I noticed Smudge was cocooned in her igloo. Oh, good I thought, she can't be kittening yet as cats do like privacy for that. But then, I was dealing with Smudge, not your average cat…if there is such a thing.

After we returned to the house I made tea and the usual home bakes, taking them through to the living room to entertain the girl and her family who were very impressed with Troubie. From the moment we sat down, Smudge began an incessant stalking of every move I made, desperately looking up into my face, then walking to the visitors to stare at them. She kept indicating to follow her back to the kitchen, then she just hopped into her igloo and lay there in the neatly fitting alcove beside the stove. Soon she was back in the living room staring at me again.

The family were comfortable, the cakes good, and time passed, with Smudge getting more and more agitated. I kept following her and offering water, food, treats, but all she did was get back into the igloo, leaving Fox hanging there on the outside.

Eventually she came back to the living room, leapt on to the arm of the chair where the girl was sitting, opened her mouth wide and spat loudly into the child's face. They were shocked. I wasn't. It dawned on me at last.

'I know this sounds kind of peculiar, but I'm going to have to ask you to...sort of, em, leave.'

'Pardon?' the mother mouthed, while the father calmed the child who said she didn't like cats.' I didn't blame her.

I tried again, but my thoughts were really of Smudge now so I just came out with it. 'The cat wants to have her kittens.' There, I said it.

This left them open mouthed. Oh, they said they understood, but we never heard from them again! Any interest in Troubie was gone.

The minute the door closed behind them, Smudge got into the igloo with what I swear was a satisfied look on her face. I wagged my finger at her, 'This better be for real, girl,' and soon she started to strain. This went on, and off, for an hour while I sweated blood. No one else was around. I'd never seen a kitten born and I felt sick with worry. If I moved from in front of the igloo, she trailed after me, so I stayed put.

Then, after a terribly long time, a black tail appeared. Nothing else, only the tail. Had this breech presentation been a lamb, I'd know what to do. But a kitten? I was sick with worry, and no matter how she strained, nothing else came.

Right, I thought, she may be just a moggie but she's my moggie and I love her so I'm phoning the vet. I explained the situation, in a voice shaking with anxiety. Dead silence. 'Will I take her in?'

'Oh, that won't be necessary...'

'Will you call then?' I cut in, knowing that was a bit over the top. They really did have a busy practice, but I firmly believed my cat was in trouble.

'Leave the cat alone. Cats kitten for themselves and I can't believe Smudge is needing a midwife!' Then I heard a muffled discussion before he got back and said in a very patient, kind voice, 'Give her time, and peace to get on with it, but call me back if she really cannot deliver her kittens.' It was close on two decades ago. Today, I think I would have been told, 'Bring her in!'

Cat at foot, staring up at me, only the tail hanging out, back we went to the igloo, me sitting on the floor, her straining. I tried gently pulling the tiny wet tail but it didn't seem to help and I was terrified to interfere further. On the point of bundling her up and heading for the vet without a phone call, a little bum appeared followed by the back legs. I actually cried with relief. It was horribly alarming. In no time a tiny black and white kitten got its first wash. I went to move. Smudge got up, so back to sitting on the floor. When I relayed the drama to Connie, she sighed. 'What did you expect? It was a black and white kitten, awkward from the day they're born.' What could I say. I was beginning to believe her.

My niece Lorna's 11 year old daughter Charlene had spent her summer holiday with us, making friends with Katrina, Connie and Smudge, and hearing of the impending birth, pled with her mother for one of the kittens. If Smudge had a black and white girl kitten, she It was to be called Chi-Chi and my three grand-nieces would have her.

So Chi-Chi had safely arrived. I only just recovered when a beautiful, fluffy white and grey kitten followed, bigger than Chi-Chi. I was so relieved he came in a natural position, putting all my fears away, I happily called him Serendipity.

This time I stayed put, Smudge pretty busy settling the two kittens to a teat each. Then a white and brown stripy head appeared followed by the biggest, wettest, fluffiest feet I ever saw, except of course on a Hobbit. So The Hobbit he became. He was the living spit image of Smudge's boyfriend, her companion now for some time. He was pronounced the father and became known as The Daddy Cat.

All settled down nicely. In a photo taken then you can actually see the big smile on Smudge's face. Honestly! Three kittens were happily feeding and I was free to get back up on to my feet and get on with things. Debbie, Himself's niece would get Serendipity, so already two were promised good homes.

I felt inordinately proud, until an anxious cat came after me, a look of intense concern on her face. She rushed back to the igloo, me behind her, worried something was wrong with the kittens, but no, they were sleeping peacefully. Then she started to strain.

Out popped a really tiny white kitten with grey striped splodges, a dark grey helmet and long stripy grey tail. She was the living image of Poodie, the cat my father was devoted to at the time he so suddenly took a massive stroke, at the age of 65, only a couple of years into his hard-earned retirement. His coma was deep and lasted a traumatic two weeks before he died. It was a shocking loss and his was the biggest funeral ever held at that time in our area.

I called this kitten Poodie, after the cat that was left to greet us each time we visited Kirtomy where our devastated mother kept the family home going until suddenly, on Christmas Day 1993, twenty years later, she took a similar stroke in the middle of telling an amusing story while sitting round Sandra's dinner table, enjoying the company. She died instantly. Both our parents had left their Kirtomy home in good spirits, never to return again, both dying suddenly of the same condition.

Poodie eventually got dubbed Poodie-Pooh but I feared for her survival that first hour of her life. She was so scrawny and vulnerable and each time she crawled up her mother's tummy looking for a teat, the established kittens kicked her off. Who was this usurper? I'm sure if I hadn't been acting midwife they'd have let her starve, but I sat there ensuring she got her milk, albeit from the least productive teat on offer, and her siblings made sure she stuck with that teat, demanding their rights even before they were two hours old. But she showed them. She came back fighting, asserting her right to life.

And taking a leaf out of her book, so did I!